Rooms
for recreation

Euan Barty

a Design Centre book

Rooms for recreation
First edition published 1977
A Design Centre book published by
Design Council 28 Haymarket
London SW1Y 4SU

Designed by Anne Fisher
Printed and bound by Balding + Mansell Ltd
London and Wisbech

ISBN 0 85072 054 0 (paperback)
ISBN 0 85072 055 9 (hardback)
©Euan Barty 1976

Contents

Introduction

Plenty of books tell you how to make dresses, brew your own beer, weave rugs and so on, but surprisingly few of them take any time at all to tell you how to choose and plan an appropriate room for your hobby.

This is an attempt to put that right, although 'suggest' would be a more suitable word than 'tell'. It cannot be a comprehensive book, of course, either in the hobbies it covers or in the range of advice it gives. The hope is that by applying some basic principles, which are outlined in the first part of the book, to a number of common activities described in the later sections, it will spark off ideas with a wider application than just the context in which they appear.

There is no avoiding the tendency to talk in terms of solutions that may seem ludicrously idealistic and up-market when set against your own problems and budget. But at least the 'ideal' solution gives you an idea of what a compromise should be aiming at. And wherever possible I have included low-cost alternatives to the more inflationary suggestions.

There is some confusion these days over what is the length, width, depth or height of a worktop, shelf, drawer or sink. Throughout this book I have used length to mean the distance from end to end, width to mean the distance from side to side (often called 'depth' in relation to shelves etc), depth to mean the distance from top downwards (eg from the rim of a sink to its base), and height to mean the distance from bottom upwards, in most cases starting from the floor. All dimensions are given either in metric originals or metricated equivalents.

I feel drawn to apologise for the use of the word 'hobby' throughout the book, on account of its Boy Scout-ish overtones. But if you think about it there is really no other word that quite captures the middle ground between the professionalism of 'occupation' and the anaemia of 'interest'.

My thanks to Robert Matthew, Johnson-Marshall & Partners, Edinburgh, for the use of their excellent library; and to my wife for her many comments, based as they were on an astoundingly dilettant-ish experience of almost every hobby in the book.

Part One
General planning

Making room

For a few people picking up this book, the section that follows will be irrelevant; they are the lucky ones who already have a room available that can be completely given over to their hobbies. For the rest, finding or making space may be the most difficult part of the whole exercise.

The amount of space you need varies with the hobby. Most of the 'dirty' activities in Part Three need rooms to themselves, whereas for the less rugged pursuits in Part Two some compromise is often possible. In most cases they could double up, at least with a spare bedroom. More detail on dual-purpose rooms in the next section.

Studies, in particular, do not need rooms to themselves, unless the need to work undisturbed is very great. It is sufficient to hive off a corner of another room (preferably not the living room). In older houses especially, seek out odd alcoves that could be pressed into service. How long is it, for instance, since you looked creatively at the cupboard under the stairs? A small desk, a chair, some localised lighting and a bit of wall storage can often be shoe-horned in. It will feel less cramped if you take out the side wall, extend the hall carpet into the alcove, and finish the back of the stairs in timber panelling or painted plywood.

Where more space is required, the first question to ask yourself is whether the existing space is being fully exploited. In general it will prove cheaper to modify an existing building than to add to it, and integral improvements tend to add more to the value of the house than extensions (they add to the rates too, of course). The first place to look is the loft.

Converting a loft into one room can cost up to £3000, and into two or more £4000–£5000, but even at these prices it is probably the cheapest way of getting an extra room. If you are ever likely to want more than one room in the roof space, build the partitions in from the start, but don't be misled by apparently huge spaces in the loft – up to 40 per cent of the floor area may be virtually unusable because of the slope of the roof.

It is possible to go it alone with a builder who specialises in loft conversions, as long as the project is straightforward and doesn't involve any structural alterations. Otherwise you should employ an architect and not be shy about cross-examining him if you do not understand his plans and think that, in any case, it could all be a good bit cheaper.

Planning permission is not necessary if the ridge line of the roof is not raised and new windows are not inserted. Most architects look for at least 2500mm in height at the ridge if it is not to be raised, but this is not an essential requirement – it depends on how much standing will be done in the converted room. On the one hand, don't let yourself in for a lot of stooping, but on the other try to avoid structural alterations if at all possible, not only to side-step planning difficulties but because they add enormously to the cost.

If the room is classified as 'habitable' (a study/bedroom for instance), building and fire regulations become rather onerous, and the latter especially may make your plans impossibly expensive particularly if they change a two-storey building into a three-storey one. They include, for instance, a minimum 2286mm headroom over at least the floor area, and a fixed stair rising at an angle of not more than 42 degrees. However, the chances are that a leisure room will not be classed as habitable, and the rules for non-habitable rooms are a good deal less strict.

If you are stuck with difficult regulations, you could consider opening the loft to the floor below and then sub-dividing the height to provide the space required – in effect putting the new room on a mezzanine level. Needless to say this is a very costly idea, and you may run into unforeseen noise problems. A study above a little-used room like a dining room, though, would work quite well.

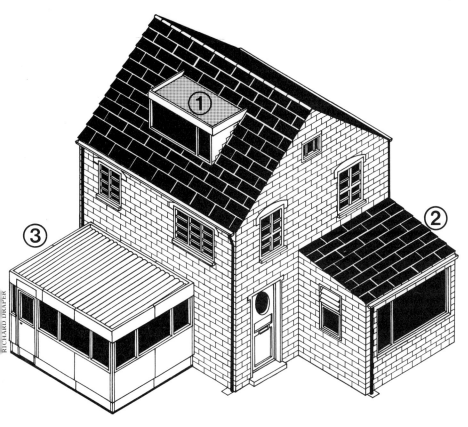

RICHARD DRAPER

Three ways of making more room.
1 *a loft conversion is probably cheapest, but it will need insulation and the sloping roof reduces the usable floor space.*
2 *a traditional, brick-built extension can match the rest of the house, but it is expensive and will need an architect.*
3 *a kit extension comes in prefabricated sections, which some makers say can be put up by a competent handyman.*

You can consider saving space beneath the trap-door by using a narrow spiral stair or a telescopic ladder instead of a fixed stair, but not if children or elderly people are to have access. You should make sure there are at least two metres of headroom at the top of whichever stair you choose, and remember to have a switch for at least one of the loft lights at the bottom of the stair.

Slate or tile roofs can be under-sealed by a specialist spray-on method, guaranteed for twenty-five years, if you are doubtful as to their weather-resistance. The inside of the roof will have to be insulated when you convert, irrespective of whether you already have insulation

laid on what will become the floor of the new room.

Builders' insulating board can be nailed directly to the underside of the rafters and then painted or papered, but make sure it provides at least 75mm of insulation. Alternatively, timber panelling is a popular finish for more expensive loft interiors, with insulating blanket inserted between the panelling and the underside of the roof. If you already have this on the loft floor, you can save a bit of money by re-using it, but it will not be enough to go round. If the loft is to be heated independently of the rest of the house, it will be snugger and more economical to leave it where it is and add new roof insulation.

Cellar conversions are strictly a minority business, because few houses nowadays have cellars. Where they do exist they can provide excellent extra rooms provided that they are bone dry. Their natural advantages include both thermal and noise insulation, constant temperature, a solid floor, easy access to plumbing, and (usually) a fixed stair.

However, where 'change of use' is involved you will need an architect to steer you through the planning jungle, the more so if you are planning a habitable room. In this case demanding building and fire regulations apply. They include a minimum height of 2286mm and very complex either/or stipulations about the relationship of window area to floor area, space outside the window, ventilation and so on. Definitely to be avoided if possible.

Damp cellars introduce new dimensions of difficulty. It is not impossible to make usable rooms out of them, but it will almost certainly be costly. Extensive use of impervious rendering can sometimes be effective, but it is not a permanent solution, and if the cellar is going to come in for serious use you will have to install a damp-proof membrane. This may be forced on you anyway by the building regulations.

If there is water pressure behind the walls, things get still more complicated and expensive; it will have to be relieved by tanking. Residual damp will limit the choice of interior finishes – possibly for years. It would probably be better to look at alternatives before letting yourself in for this.

Apart from the loft conversions already mentioned, these alternatives involve new building and divide naturally into self-contained units (the garden shed approach) and extensions. In both cases you will need planning permission if the volume of the new building exceeds 49·55 cubic metres (measured outside) or 10 per cent of the existing house, whichever is the greater, up to a maximum of 113·27 cubic metres. Anything less than this is considered 'permitted development' if it is at the back of the house.

If an extension is added to a window wall, it must not obstruct the windows unless it has adequate window space itself. It must also not interfere with existing ventilation. All inside walls must be fire-resistant, and outside ones as well if they are within 915mm of a boundary.

Don't assume you will be able to build on top of a flat-roofed garage; in many cases the foundations will not be strong enough. Be careful not to block off side access to the back of the house, or you may find yourself trekking dustbins through the hall every week. One possibility if space is tight is to build a structure on top of a semi-open car-port.

Watch out for subtle Catch-22s, though. Check the title deeds of your house first for covenants restricting or prohibiting new building. In Scotland you may have to negotiate with the holder of your feu, whether or not feu duty itself has been redeemed. If you live in a listed building or conservation area, you will need special consent even for what would ordinarily count as permitted development.

And that is not all by any means. If you are a leaseholder you must get the permission of your freeholder. If you are a mortgagee you will need the consent of your building society or equivalent (in fact, getting the building society to finance the extension can be recommended). If foundations will run under your neighbour's land, or the extension otherwise affects the boundary, more negotiation will be needed.

Basic garden sheds can be bought in kit form for do-it-yourself erection, and probably won't need planning permission, but they may not be large enough for your needs and they will require extra insulation. If your requirements, or those of the building regulations, are complex, you will most likely have to go for a purpose-designed building. Timber is usually cheaper than brick, and if you are a good handyman you will probably be able to put the building up yourself.

Red cedar is recommended for cladding, as it is naturally weather-proof and gradually turns a mellow grey. Other woods will have to be treated and painted. Exteriors will have to be periodically face-lifted. Make sure that walls and ceilings have at least 75mm of thermal insulation, either by using insulating board or by filling the cavity between the external and internal skins.

Traditional home extensions are brick-built and expensive – allow at least £160 per square metre of new floor space. Horror stories abound, and it is advisable to spend more if that is what it takes to get

If you're lucky, you will be able to find a space that can be permanently devoted to your hobby. Peter Schagen has a converted loft for his extensive model railway system. Rob Perry has a workshop in an outbuilding and his bench is a coal bunker.

9

a reputable architect and builder.

In both cases personal recommendation is about the best way of finding the right person, but architects can be more randomly located via the local RIBA branch (or RIBA's Directory – in reference libraries), and local authority architects or planning departments may be willing to tell you which architects in your area specialise in the kind of work you want. Ask architects you are considering to show you the sort of work they have done in the past, and make sure the one you choose has 'professional indemnity insurance'.

Your architect should be capable of eliminating bad risk builders, but in case he isn't, make sure he's had several quotations for the job, and not necessarily picked the cheapest – especially if it was a lot lower than the rest. Membership of the National Housebuilders Registration Council (if you can find it in a builder doing extensions) is to a certain extent a recommendation.

It is possible to save about a quarter of the building costs by skipping a builder altogether and hiring your own sub-contractors. Equally, you can reduce your architect's fee from 13 per cent of the project cost to 3 per cent by requesting a 'partial service' (ie plans only) instead of a full service. But neither of these can be recommended unless you really know what you are doing.

Apart from the risk of getting badly conned, the big problem if you do decide to be your own contractor is co-ordinating the arrival of materials and men, and getting the right specialists in the right order. You will need to supervise constantly. If you are doing this, two points to remember: have plenty of plastic sheeting for unglazed windows and doors, and hire a skip for rubble.

Kit extensions are much cheaper – between a third and a quarter of the cost of building in brick – and they usually come complete with planning and building permission. They are flexible in design (one maker offers several thousand permutations), can be put up quite quickly, and are generally fairly maintenance free.

The main disadvantage is that they look precisely what they are – cheap and prefabricated; however hard the manufacturers try to disguise this by using simulated exterior finishes, it's never very convincing. Some manufacturers say they can be put up by competent handymen, but this is a dubious claim better not put to the test.

Wherever brick is used as a building material (as for an extension or for a separate building) make sure that cavity walls are filled with insulating material as they go up. This will also help noise insulation a bit. Thermal insulation can be improved further by using insulating bricks for the inner walls, and these can be painted directly with a colour wash if you don't mind a rough-textured finish inside.

Dual-purpose rooms

Provided that two activities are reasonably compatible, they can often be accommodated in the same room. It makes sense not to confuse the two activities – make it clear how much of the room is given to each activity, and make sure they each have their own storage, for instance. It can be convenient to use room dividers (such as double-sided shelf units) in a large enough room. But there is no point trying to disguise the dual function – it will just look unconvincing.

There are too many permutations of the dual-purpose room to go into here, but some basic principles can be gleaned from looking at two rather different examples – the study/bedroom and the garage/workshop. There is also a note at the end of the section on mezzanine structures in tall rooms.

Study/bedrooms

Study/bedrooms are usually associated with teenagers, but there is no reason why any bedroom should not double up – especially the spare bedroom. It should be as far away as possible from general family hubbub, not only to aid concentration, but also to protect the family from rattling typewriters.

In most respects the interior layout can be dictated by the needs of the bedroom, with a few modifications as a concession to the secondary use. All internal finishes come into this category: a domestic carpet for instance is ideal for a study and any plain wall finish will serve (violent patterns might be distracting). Heating, however, will have to be higher than is usual in a bedroom.

Fittings and furniture for writing are discussed in Part Two, but the dual purpose may restrict choice a bit – you don't want guests to feel they're being put up in the office. You will have to decide at the outset whether the two activities should be visually integrated or visually distinct; visual integration does not mean disguise, it means carrying over colour schemes and sometimes furniture ranges so as to prevent a feeling of 'busy-ness'. The size of the room is a major influence here; generally the argument for integration in a small room is overwhelming.

Rooms in university residences are extreme examples of integrated study/bedrooms, but they do suggest ideas which you can apply to any small room, even if not quite so rigorously. Everything is pushed back against the walls, for instance, leaving as much space as possible in the centre of the room.

Related activities are grouped together so that the bed is close to the washbasin, the wardrobe and clothes drawers, allowing a logical progression when getting up and going to bed. Working surfaces, frequently-used bookshelves and deeper drawers form a coherent group by the window. For things used less often, drawers slung beneath the bed and higher-level storage use the available space well.

Clever use of localised lighting – flexible desk lamps or fixed spots – emphasises functional areas. Materials are co-ordinated and proportions related so as to minimise the cramped feeling in what is really a very small space indeed.

These, of course, are purpose-designed rooms, but the principles of space usage and co-ordination of materials and colours work just as well when applied less formally. Some makers of fitted bedroom furniture, for instance, include desk modules in their ranges and these – if they are strong enough – are cheaper than free-standing desks and easier to clean under. Alternatively, two drawer cabinets within a bedroom range could be used to support a home-made worktop.

Storage – always more than at first seems necessary – should be flexible. Shelves should be on adjustable brackets, and other units should preferably be modular ones so that they can be added, subtracted or re-located as requirements change. Colours should be closely related. If in doubt, integrate. But where a

larger, well-lit room is available, and particularly if it is the user's own bedroom, there may be something to be said for providing a clean visual break between the bed and work areas – even if only for psychological reasons.

If this is the aim, it is important that one area does not jut into the other. This is easier to achieve by, say, giving over the whole of one wall to the study so that the user's back is to the rest of the room, his working surface in front, and his storage on either side. Storage units should not protrude beyond the width of the working surface if possible, and the effect could be heightened by dividing the carpet and using a different floor covering down the length of the work area. Colours should

harmonise between the two areas and not clash, and lighting should be predominantly local rather than appearing to come from the rest of the room. In this situation, more business-like furniture is acceptable.

This study/bedroom in the University of East Anglia is a good example of rigorous planning in a small space. Architects Denys Lasdun and Partners.

Garage/workshops

Making your garage double as a workshop is one of the best ways of accommodating noisy, dirty hobbies like woodworking or metalworking, or any work with plastic resins, which have highly penetrating smells. Depending on the dimensions of your garage and car, you should have a fair bit of space at the back of the garage even when the car is in. Most garages are built to take fairly large cars, so you win space as well as saving money if you trade down.

The big problem of the garage/workshop is that it tends to be cold and, when the car is parked, inaccessible. It should be possible to carve a door in one of the side walls at the workshop end, however, and if you have space on both sides of the garage, a second one opposite can be convenient when manoeuvring long pieces of material. It can also provide extra light and ventilation.

Whether it is worth insulating the whole garage to keep the workshop end warm is a question that could only be answered with reference to the amount you are likely to use the workshop. If it doesn't seem worth the cost, it will have to be largely a fair-weather place, though a wall-mounted radiant electric bar can help on borderline days.

The general lighting inside most garages will be inadequate and will have to be replaced, at least at the workshop end, as well as being augmented by local lighting in the work area and over machines. Rooflights can be installed over the workshop end in a flat-roofed garage; otherwise narrow windows can be let into the back wall just above the workbench, and the rafters used for storing materials.

Most garages have solid concrete floors, which makes them practical, if a little uncomfortable over long periods. Some people feel tempted to use duckboarding, partly for comfort and partly to keep their feet out of shavings etc. This is not recommended on safety grounds. A much better plan is to lay a level screed on the concrete at the workshop end and then use this as the base for sheet or tile vinyl, the foam-backed variety for more comfort. But see also the note on welding in the section on workshops in Part Three, pages 58 and 59.

Mezzanines

Lastly, a form of dual-purpose use of space for people in older houses with high ceilings – the mezzanine conversion. To build in a mezzanine platform you really need a height of about 4570mm in the original room, though you could get away with as little as 3650mm if taller people are warned to duck.

Mezzanines are most often built in a natural timber like pine, but an interesting and quite cheap alternative is to build a framework out of steel or aluminium tube scaffolding and paint it an appropriate colour. Although this sounds delightfully simple, professional advice should be taken on floor loadings and safety aspects. Local building regulations may apply.

A mezzanine platform should not cover more than about a third of the original room's floor area or it will become overpowering, especially if a shallow stair is used instead of a spiral. This somewhat restricts its uses (though a room tall enough to accommodate a mezzanine will normally have quite a large area too), but a mezzanine study above a living room, bedroom, or even an entrance hall, can be an ingenious use of space.

Beware, though: you are sure to run into trouble with the fire regulations if you try to put a bedroom on the mezzanine platform, because access is not allowed through a 'day room'. Thus you can have a non-habitable room such as, say, a jewellery workshop over a bedroom, but not vice versa. Also, there is a catch in all this: houses with enough room to accommodate mezzanines often turn out to be listed buildings or in conservation areas, and this means there are restrictions on internal as well as external developments, so planning consent will be needed.

With a large garage, or a small car, there may be room for a general workshop like this one. Ideally, there will be a door through from the house and room to store materials on ceiling and wall racks. Extra lighting will be essential and narrow windows above the workbench are valuable too.

Working surfaces

It is reasonable to suppose that you will be spending many hours at your desk, workbench or whatever, so it is important that you should be comfortable at it. Unfortunately many people have not the slightest inkling of the factors that contribute to, or detract from, comfort in working postures.

Consumerists always say that you should test furniture in the shop before you buy it, but really this can only eliminate the totally unsuitable. Sitting in a chair for a couple of minutes will tell you whether it bulges where it should unquestionably give, but it will not tell you whether a chair that feels fine at that point will continue to do so after a couple of hours at the sewing machine.

Even the experts – ergonomists and (wait for it) anthropometrists – periodically change their minds on quite fundamental calculations. Still, it is possible to mention a few basic points that you should bear in mind when choosing or making your furniture.

Seated activities
Enshrined in a British Standard, 430mm above the ground has become a popular height for office seating, and if this is right for you (as it is for a large proportion of the population) it will simplify the choice of both seating and desk, since the two are often related.

Most people know what to look for in a comfortable chair – firm support in the lumbar region of the back, under the buttocks, and along the underside of the thighs when the legs are planted at 90 degrees to the floor. People who are slightly too tall for the standard chair will not suffer badly, as it is physiologically less wearing to endure a seat that is too low than one that is too high. Very tall and very small people will have to shop around quite a bit, though – or resort to such tactics as blocking up or cutting down the legs of chair or desk.

Adjustable typists' chairs (into which a great deal of ergonomic research has gone) may overcome some of these problems. If they are going to be used at a high setting, make sure they have an adequate footrest.

Proprietary desk heights are usually between 650–750mm (700mm is popular with manufacturers of modular office furniture ranges). Once upon a time it was thought suitable to establish an angle of 20 degrees downwards between the elbow and the working surface, but tests on young adults by the Department of Education and Science suggest that elbow height itself is more comfortable, provided that this is the height at which the actual work takes place (not necessarily the height of the worktop itself).

As a rule of thumb, drop the working surface 100mm to take account of the height of sewing machine bases, typewriter keyboards etc. If you have to use the same worktop for two or more activities with distinctly different heights, let the worktop height be dictated by the activity that adds most to it (ie choose the lower worktop height). The only exception to this rule is when finicky work needs to be carried out at or just below eye level; you should make separate provision for this.

Standing activities
Standing worktops should also be related to elbow height, and the same recommendation applies – the actual work should be carried out at elbow height. Of course, actual working heights will vary from hour to hour, but dropping the work surface 100mm beneath the elbow will accommodate a large number of small-to-medium jobs; this is the height implied by the expression 'general worktop' when it is used in later sections of this book.

There are specific exceptions here, though. The first is when the work demands considerable downward pressure (such as wedging clay for pottery). If this is only momentary, the general worktop height will be adequate, but if it is a continual feature of the work, the surface would be better 200mm below the elbow to allow the full weight of the body to be exerted through the arms. This would be uncomfortably low for a general worktop, however, so if possible a separate surface should be reserved for this kind of activity.

The second exception is where there are long periods during which fine, detailed work needs to be carried out close to the eyes. If the general worktop is used, it means bending the trunk right over the work in a back-breaking position.

The better solution is to have a separate worktop, or part of a worktop, which is related to eye level rather than the elbows. The job should be within 300mm of the eyes when the body is relaxed and the head facing downwards. Although the hands will then be well above elbow height, this will not be uncomfortable if no force is being applied. For long-term work of this kind, however, it is usually better to sit – either at a convenient table and chair, or on a stool or adjustable typists' chair to lower the body till the eyes are at the right height above the general worktop.

Then there is larger volume work, in which pieces of wood, sculpture or metalwork, say, may stand 600mm or more above the worktop. The temptation to lower the worktop accordingly is not necessarily a sound one, however. Despite the size of the total work, you may spend quite a lot of time working on parts of it near the base. However, the height suggested above for downward pressure (200mm below the elbows) would be a fair compromise.

For most work, a maximum width of 400mm is satisfactory while worktop length is most often dictated by space available. In certain specific circumstances rather large working surfaces are needed; these are pointed out later in the appropriate sections in Parts Two and Three.

Sinks

Sinks should be regarded as working surfaces in a category of their own. Their problem is the relationship between rim height and sink depth: too high a rim makes it difficult to lift things in and out; too low a sink bottom means uncomfortable bending. Research indicates that rim height should be about 25mm below elbow height for average kitchen sinks, and this can be used as a guide for special-purpose shallow sinks (as used in darkrooms) as well. This means, of course, that the rim will often be higher than surrounding work surfaces – an implication ignored for aesthetic reasons by makers of fitted kitchen furniture.

Second-hand furniture

In some sections in Parts Two and Three, buying second-hand furniture from junk-shops has been recommended, especially where worktops are liable to come in for rough treatment and money is better saved for expensive equipment or materials. Junk-shop furniture tends to date from an age when ergonomics was a gleam in the eye, and is unlikely to be found bespoke, as it were. So be prepared to block up worktops, or stand them on plinths if they are too low, or even (unlikely) saw them down if they are too high: a safer way of adjusting the worktop to the body than standing on duckboards.

Storage

One of the cardinal rules in planning a leisure room is to have as much storage as possible. Most people underestimate their storage requirements, either because guessing is hard in this rather nebulous area, or because they use their present needs as their criteria instead of future ones. Arbitrarily doubling your first guess will not prove far wrong.

What kind of storage you need varies from hobby to hobby and is dealt with more fully in Parts Two and Three. With a few exceptions (possibly studies, certainly study/bedrooms) aesthetics are a low priority in a leisure room. Look for low cost and high versatility.

Open shelving satisfies both these criteria, and for most purposes will be satisfactory, although closed storage space may be necessary to protect against dust or excessive light or heat. Shelves on cantilevered brackets which can be moved up and down vertical wall fittings are more versatile than fixed bracket shelves, and are recommended. The brackets should be inset, not right at the ends of the shelves, and the shelves themselves sealed with polyurethane or painted to keep them clean.

You should allow frequency of use to dictate the height at which you store different objects and space the shelves accordingly, regardless of whether this destroys their symmetry. Things that are often used should be stored at heights between 700–1400mm. Light objects in fairly frequent use should be stored in bands about 500–700mm and 1400–1900mm above the floor. Spaces beneath the 500mm and above the 1900mm levels should be kept for rarely used items. Obviously these figures are only a guide – they will vary with each person's height, and should be reduced if you are reaching over a worktop.

Make sure that the shelves are wide enough for your needs, remembering that the depth you will be able to reach decreases as the shelves get higher and that this decrease will be greater if they are over a worktop. Unless you have a good memory, there is little point storing things where you can't see them, so angle of vision will have a bearing on shelf planning.

Frequency of use works horizontally as well as vertically. Storage space nearest to the working area should be kept for tools and materials most frequently used, and for things which may be used less often but need to be seized in a hurry when they are wanted. Group functionally related objects together so that you don't have to walk round the room collecting different tools for a single job.

Try as you may, groups of objects on shelves will tend to run into each other, and you will quickly feel the need for some sort of divider. Labelled box files are the best answer for papers, transparent plastic boxes are good for small items like nails and screws. Purpose-designed containers tend to be developed for every conceivable article. Sometimes these are useful, like paint boxes, but often they could be copied much more cheaply with a little ingenuity. Plastic-coated wire trays, washing-up bowls, buckets, and drawers slung beneath worktops make adequate general-purpose containers and can be colour-coded for extra ease of identification. The ultimate low-cost solution is to beg orange boxes from a grocer, scrub them, and stand them on their sides. But watch out for splinters and odd nails – sanding them down will help.

16

JESSICA STRANG

Adequate storage is essential in any work-room.
Left: a system of wire baskets and shelves keeps materials on view and close at hand.
Above: orange boxes from a friendly greengrocer are a cheap alternative.
Right: plastic storage units are useful in a study or drawing office. Here they are hung from clamps on ceiling joists and can easily be moved around as necessary.
Far right: this 'cupboard office' can be completely hidden away when not in use. The doors are fitted with shelves and clips to hold files and papers.

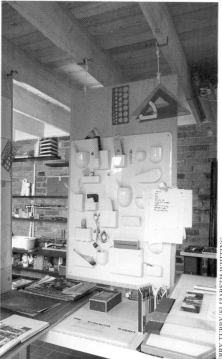

JERRY TUBBY/ELIZABETH WHITING

TIM STREET-PORTER/ELIZABETH WHITING

Vertical storage makes a lot of sense in workshops and similar places – pegboard hooks and clips are ideal for tools. But the same principle can be adapted for use in a study or drawing office, with shallow pockets of different sizes used for magazines, papers, pens, rulers and so on. Again, purpose-designed units are available in plastics, but heavy-duty paper bags reinforced round the top with tape and glued to a suitable backing board will do the job, and at next to no cost.

Where drawer and cupboard space is essential (such as in a sewing room), consider units in a modular range of storage which can be shifted round, added or (less likely) subtracted as the need arises. This not only provides functional flexibility but it eliminates the need for guessing maximum storage requirements in advance. This in turn can even out expenditure in a useful way.

If space is at a premium, you may have difficulty fitting in all the storage you require. Look for hitherto redundant spaces that can be used for storing things you won't need often, thus alleviating pressure elsewhere. Under worktops and above and around doors, for instance. An efficient, but rather expensive, way of using corner space is to buy a revolving unit from a range of fitted kitchen furniture. Any box, chest or drawer unit that has to be hidden away under a worktop will be more easily retrieved if it is on castors.

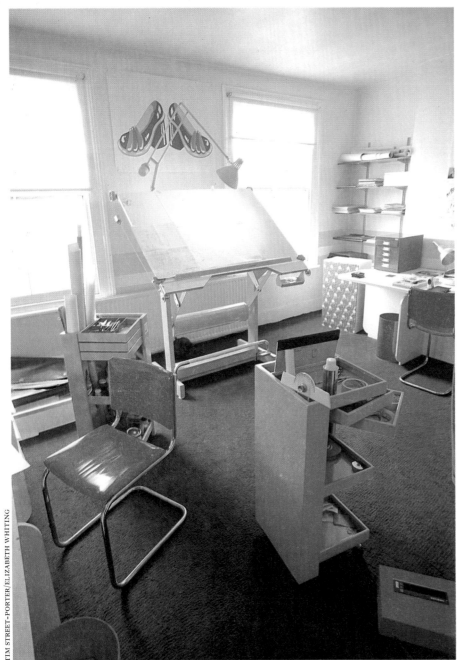

Lighting

Good light is vital to almost all hobbies, and for some it may be the main criterion in choosing and planning a room. The requirements are rather different from elsewhere in the home – more illumination is needed, avoidance of shadow and glare is a matter of safety and accuracy rather than comfort, and aesthetics are comparatively unimportant.

The recommended level of light for work areas is 400 lux (lumens per square metre) in most cases, but it should be 600 lux for minute detailed operations like sewing, jewellery and some model-making. Calculating the wattage required to give these levels is fairly complex, but as a comparison the recommended level for kitchens and light reading is 200 lux, for living rooms, halls and stairs 100 lux, and for garages and bedrooms 50 lux. The subject is covered in more detail in *Planning your lighting* by Derek Phillips, one of the other books in this series.

Daylight is many times superior in power and quality to anything man has yet come up with, and it is also free. It should therefore be exploited at every opportunity. On an average day, the area just inside a window will yield more than 900 lux, so it follows that placing work surfaces close to a window will guarantee sufficient light during the day except when the weather is very bad. It is generally better to work sideways on to a window rather than facing it, to avoid glare and the chance of your equipment shadowing the work in hand.

Plenty of daylight, supplemented by an adjustable cantilevered lamp fixed to the drawing table, helps to make this small drawing office bright and cheerful as well as efficient – a good recipe for any workroom.

Ideally the background to the work should be about one-third as bright as the work itself, and visible surroundings should never fall to less than 10 per cent. In most rooms the natural fall-off of light intensity as you move back from the window provides these conditions, but in some rooms with only one window which is small in relation to the room size, the far end of the room may be only 5 per cent as bright as the area next to the window.

Some of the inherent disadvantages of daylight – its inflexibility and its tendency to use up valuable wall space – can be countered without recourse to electricity. In lofts and single-storey structures, for instance, well planned rooflights can provide a good general level of light, with less likelihood of being overshadowed, and leaving the walls free for storage.

Rooflights should have 45 degree cut-offs to prevent glare, and incorporate a ventilator or open mechanically if there is no other good source of fresh air. Adjustable blinds of the louvre or pinoleum kind can be used to stop direct sunlight overheating the room. Double-glazing prevents condensation and provides insulation, but at a price (see next section).

Light provided by a conventional window can be boosted in more distant parts of the room by using light-coloured finishes for ceilings, walls and floors – respectively about 70, 30, and 15 per cent efficient at reflection. As a last resort, large mirrors can be used to help.

There is no point making an issue out of daylight if you cannot keep the windows clean, and this problem becomes more pressing the higher above the ground your leisure room is. Unless you are going to rely on rain, therefore, don't install a rooflight until you have worked out how to clean it. Window-cleaners' ladders do not usually reach to more than three storeys. Windows that swivel on a central axis can be turned almost inside out for cleaning, and these are good for upper-storey rooms and lofts. But make sure before you buy that the window does swivel through something approaching 180 degrees, or you will have a lot of dangerous stretching to do.

Next to daylight, fluorescent tubes give the best general lighting, almost free of shadow, and at two or three times the efficiency of tungsten bulbs of the same wattage. Unless some other suggestion is made in the sections that follow, they are recommended for all leisure rooms. Their drawback in normal domestic use – that they seem harsh and clinical – matters less in a working area. They should be suspended, mounted or recessed well above eye level to avoid glare. Bare tubes are not recommended – they should be cased in plastic diffusers.

Many fluorescents – unfortunately including the highest-efficiency commercial tubes – are deficient in red light. This need not be a drawback in many cases, but where acute colour judgement is needed (as in painting, dyeing, some sculpture and some needlework) insist on an accurately balanced tube. 'Colour 27 de luxe warm white' (not the confusingly similar 'warm white') or the daylight-simulating 'colour 34 natural' are the ones to go for. Ask to see the tube in action before you buy it, and reject it if you can see the flicker.

In a small room a single fluorescent tube suspended directly above the work-top may provide enough light for that area and the rest of the room as well. For instance, a 1500mm 80W fluorescent tube with a plastic reflector fitted 1370mm above a worktop will shed 430 lux directly beneath.

Normally, however, it will be a waste of electricity to provide general lighting at the maximum level required at the work areas of the room. It would be better to use fluorescents to provide around 200 lux, with localised spotlights or adjustable table lamps providing the extra needed over specific areas and machines. These will also combat any residual stroboscopic effects from the fluorescents.

Most leisure rooms will be crowded enough without free-standing light fittings trailing flexes to be tripped over, so there is no place for standard lamps. Spots can be mounted permanently on walls, ceilings or continuous power tracks (which can be used to power other appliances and power tools up to 0·5 horsepower or 375W in total), retaining some flexibility. Adjustable table lamps are better held by brackets attached to horizontal or vertical surfaces or clamped to the table rather than stood on it. Spots should be at least 100W (depending on the level of illumination required and their distance from the surface) and table lamps at least 60W.

Continuous power tracks can be recommended for most leisure rooms as they take off all flexes into what may be otherwise unused space, and are more versatile than fixed sockets. They do not necessarily have to be mounted on the ceiling – under the lowest shelf above a workbench may be more appropriate.

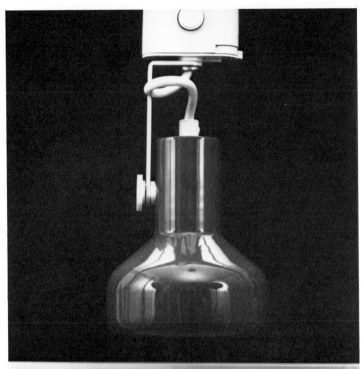

Good lighting where you need it is essential in any workroom. Lighting track is easy to install and adjust. The illustration shows Topsy spotlights on Lytespan track from Concord Lighting. Alternatively, an adjustable light such as the 1001 Lamps model (above left) can be clamped to the bench or worktop, or used with a wall bracket or table base.

Heating

Through the thicket of (sometimes contradictory) advice, recommendations, codes of practice, standards and even legal minima that surrounds the question of room temperatures, one simple fact shines like a beacon – different people feel comfortable at different temperatures.

If this is not a sufficient reason to avoid generalising on leisure rooms, there are another two. The amount of physical activity involved in hobbies varies greatly from one hobby to another and sometimes between two people doing the same thing. And the environment may become quite considerably affected by heat from machines used intermittently like kilns, irons, electric rings and butane torches.

For all these reasons, the first recommendation for heating leisure rooms is flexibility. Where 'physical' hobbies are concerned, your choice of heating system should be capable of providing room temperatures at least between 13° and 16°C. The corresponding range for more sedentary activities is 18–22°C. Experiment until you find the heat that suits you best, remembering that cold hands are not only uncomfortable but less sensitive (and hence less accurate and safe) than warm ones.

Central heating is ideal for many leisure rooms and if it is thermostatically controlled it will adjust itself should a heat-generating appliance raise the room temperature. It may be possible to extend an existing central heating system to a converted loft or extension without overtaxing the boiler: check with the supplier. If not, it is not likely to be worth upgrading the whole system for the sake of one extra room unless it is going to be in constant use.

If there is a need for constant background heat, not necessarily at a very high temperature (to prevent tools rusting, for example), a small night-storage heater, a low-wattage (250–500W) convector or a flueless gas convector would be suitable.

This will not be necessary if an otherwise unheated room is within the shell of a centrally heated house.

In home extensions and new buildings, underfloor heating provides a comfortable glow without the 'layered' effect produced by some other types of heating that cause the head to be much warmer than the feet. It is also less desiccating than central heating. It is good with hard floors like quarry tiles, timber (laid on concrete) and cork, vinyl or linoleum, but it should not be used with fitted carpets. Low-temperature radiant ceiling panels are an alternative for new structures, but like underfloor heating they are expensive to install in existing houses.

For rooms that do not require to be heated at all when they are not in use, the prime requirement is for a quick response to keep warming-up times to the minimum. Fan heaters provide this best, and if thermostatically controlled will maintain a constant temperature, cutting themselves out when a heat-generating appliance is used. Thermostatically controlled gas radiant convectors also provide a fairly fast response, but need flues. Wall-mounted electric radiant heaters provide fast response in their immediate area, but heat a whole room fairly slowly.

Whether it is better to burn electric space heaters at the domestic tariff while you actually use the room, or to maintain a constant heat using off-peak tariffs, depends entirely on how often you use the room, and for how long at a time. It is a calculation that only you can make, but examine the costs carefully. Off-peak heating is no longer the bargain it used to be.

Safety

Open fires, paraffin and oil heaters, and portable electric radiant fires are not recommended for leisure rooms for safety reasons. If they absolutely have to be used, establish a 'no-go area' of 900mm around them – they should be outside your circulation area within the room, and that distance from any furniture, materials or equipment. Paraffin heaters are unsuitable for rooms where metal tools are in use, as the very high humidity they create promotes rust. Closed solid-fuel appliances are an improvement on open fires from the safety angle, but they will still need stoking and one of the points about heating in a leisure room is that it should be something which doesn't distract you.

Insulation

Whatever your choice of heating, you should maximise its efficiency by thoroughly insulating the building. The principles have been so much rehearsed in the last few years that everyone should know them by now – filling the gaps in cavity walls with foam, a 75mm thick blanket of glass fibre or mineral wool in the roof, draught excluders fitted to doors and windows, and so on. Double glazing has been oversold, however – it is expensive relative to the savings it provides, and lined curtains go a long way towards achieving the same effect. A sheet of aluminium foil glued to walls behind radiators can help their output.

Ventilation

Two air changes an hour are recommended for leisure rooms. Permanent ventilation points are especially important for non-electric heaters of all kinds – it is not enough to rely on gaps under doors or in floorboards. Where toxic or noisome materials like acids, glues, resins etc are used, ordinary ventilation is inadequate. Wide open windows are satisfactory in summer, but a mechanical extractor will be required in cold weather. Doors connecting the room with other parts of the house should be sealed to exclude fumes.

Walls and floors

For hobbies in Part Two, the whole range of domestic wall and floor coverings is suitable unless specific exceptions are made in individual sections. The activities are unlikely to involve spillage, splashes, dust accumulation or dirt above the average, so there is no objection to such otherwise vulnerable choices as carpet for the floor and wallpaper or emulsion paint for the walls.

The main thing is simply that it should be a room you enjoy being in. Conceivably, dropped needles may be fractionally easier to find on, say, vinyl than on carpet, but this is nit-picking. Hard floor coverings will usually seem out of place.

One or two constraints are worth bearing in mind, though. Light coloured floors and walls reflect light, which may be useful (see section on lighting). Bold patterns may be distracting to the concentration, and so may outstanding contrasts between different colours. Pastel colours tend to be more self-effacing than primaries.

Aesthetics play a limited part in most leisure rooms. The room wants to be as comfortable as the body demands and the pocket allows, but it doesn't have to impress visitors. So don't spend money – unless it's going begging – on expensive carpeting. A light domestic quality carpet will be sufficient for sedentary hobbies. Apart from the question of reflection, light carpets show up dirt faster, but dark ones show up specks more obviously.

Tufted carpet is cheaper than other forms, and it comes with its own foam backing and so needs no underlay. Cheap cords wear well (some of them also have their own backing) though the colours seem curiously difficult to match. Sisal is very hard-wearing, needs little maintenance, and is also cheap. Rush matting is comparable in price with sisal and sheds dust easily. An alternative to buying anything at all is to sand down the floorboards and finish them with a poly-urethane sealer or, more adventurously, paint. This is functional, reflects light well, but may seem a little cold. Sealed cork tiles combine warmth, durability, ease of maintenance and a certain amount of insulation. They also absorb sound, which may help if there are a lot of hard surfaces in the room.

When it comes to the hobbies in Part Three, the choice is more limited. Carpet is out wherever paints, dyes, glues, clay, oil, wax or chemicals occur, and it's best avoided even if it is only water that may be splashed about.

For some of these activities, notably dyeing, pottery and some sculpture, it is an advantage to have an impermeable floor sloping very slightly to a central or side gutter and drain. It can then be sluiced down with abandon and left to dry in the air. This kind of floor is fairly easy to install in a new building or extension, but more complicated in an existing house. Brick, quarry, non-slip ceramic tiles and slate (if you can afford it) are ideal for this purpose; concrete or asphalt adequate but depressing. Sheet vinyl or linoleum will do if well coved at the edges of the room, but both tend to be slippery when wet. Synthetic sheet rubber is another possibility, though it too is slippery in the wet; natural rubber is vulnerable to oils.

If sluicing is out of the question, these rooms and most of the others in Part Three (but not woodwork or modelling rooms) should be able to withstand regular scrubbing. Any hard floor covering comes into this category except plain timber. Foam-backed vinyl is somewhat more comfortable than the plain plastic, but if you are laying vinyl tiles yourself it's easier to use the self-adhesive kind.

If you opt for an expensive but pleasant finish like quarry tiles, you will probably feel you must keep it clean. On the other hand, if you would rather not spend the time or are fatalistic about the floor's chances, choose something cheaper that can eventually be replaced (like vinyl) or simply covered (like concrete), especially if you think the room may change its function at some future date.

Walls are something of a problem up to about shoulder height, though less so higher up. A tough, polyurethane gloss paint is serviceable, but around sinks and worktops it is better to have a waterproof, corrosion-resistant finish like ceramic tiles, or laminated plastics. Vinyl wall tiles, or floor tiles for that matter, do just as well in most cases. If water-based liquids are the only threat, washable wallcoverings can be considered.

In relation to both walls and floors, be careful to check carefully with your supplier for specific vulnerability of different finishes to certain acids, alkalis, resins or other chemicals that you know you will be using.

Plumbing

Quite a few hobbies need regular access to a sink, and even when it isn't strictly necessary it is often a convenience. It is impossible to generalise about the cost of extending the household plumbing – it can vary from surprisingly cheap to dauntingly expensive according to all sorts of factors.

However there are various ways in which, to a greater or lesser extent, you can help to bring down the cost. You can, for instance, buy a second-hand sink and taps quite cheaply from a junk-shop (anything from a quarter to a tenth of the cost of new, if you hunt determinedly) and just hire a plumber to fit them. Or, using helpful features in do-it-yourself magazines, you may feel confident enough to do the job yourself.

Think about whether you need hot and cold, or just cold water. It will be a good bit cheaper to stick to cold, but on the other hand if you are ever likely to want a hot supply in the future, it will be cheaper to have it installed at the same time. Alternatives to extending the central water-heating system include 'instant' gas or electric water heaters or storage ones, mounted either on the wall above the sink, or (if large capacity) standing on the floor. Whether these will in fact work out cheaper is a complex calculation that only you can make, taking into account such factors as whether you are on a White Meter, the capacity of your hot tank or boiler, the cost of extending the central hot-water supply in your case, the possibility of picking up one of these heaters second-hand, and so on.

If you have decided on a cold supply only, think about whether it is worth having a sink at all. In some cases the water is needed only for filling large vessels and perhaps sluicing down the floor, in which case a stand-pipe above a small floor drain will be brutal but cheap. But again, it will probably be cheaper to do the whole job now if you are ever going to need a sink there rather than having to add it later.

You will almost certainly need a good-sized sink, if you need one at all, and this should outweigh aesthetic considerations in the first instance, except where you are thinking about a dual-purpose room. A standard kitchen fitting in stainless steel is often ideal if you can afford it, but before you settle, think hard about its uses. If you will be doing a lot of washing up of moulds or vessels (for candle-making or home brewing for example), you will save yourself aggravation by getting a double drainer.

If you are likely to be filling tall vessels with water, make sure you have pillar taps or a wall-mounted set at least 400mm from the bottom of the sink. An easily removed piece of hose will prevent splashing at other times with high taps.

The choice of taps is largely personal. Mixer taps have only one protruberance over the sink instead of two, but are lower than pillar taps unless wall-mounted separately. The outlet can sometimes swivel, which may be an advantage. If the cold supply is from the mains, a mixer unit will have to be the compromise version that delivers two separate jets from the same outlet (not a real mixer tap at all).

Spray taps are highly economical, and can sometimes be thermostatically controlled to produce a fixed temperature (useful, perhaps, for things like developing colour photographs); on the other hand, you may find the flow somewhat anaemic. Taps that incorporate the turning mechanism in the outlet are no good if you want to attach any kind of hose, and can be fiddly when filling tall vessels. If you can get hold of them, lever-operated 'hospital' taps can be manipulated with the arm or elbow if the hands are full or filthy. These are recommended.

Whether you have a free-standing sink (as in many bathrooms) or one built into a worktop (as in most kitchens) depends on where it stands in relation to other activities. Either way, if the space beneath is boxed in, it will be useful for storage. The ideal height for the rim of a sink is 25mm beneath the elbow, which makes it slightly higher than the 'general worktop'. This may look clumsy, but it does have the advantage of preventing you from accidentally sweeping breakables into the sink. However, if you buy a double drainer, you may have no choice but to let it in flush with the worktop.

Specify insulation for hot pipes as they are installed – it will be cheaper and much less bother than doing it later.

Noise

Most people's hobbies – thank heaven – are inherently quiet, and some of those that are not (such as when they involve a repetitive but not particularly loud noise like the clacking of a typewriter or sewing machine) can be kept at bay by relegating them to a distant corner of the house. But unfortunately some workshop activities involve noise, and at volumes capable of bringing out the neighbours. What can be done to avoid this?

First of all, bear in mind that good neighbourliness is in this context not just charitable, but legal. The Noise Abatement Act applies to homes, so insulating party walls should be your first concern. Most of what follows relates to party walls, but it applies equally to other walls in the house.

There are minimum and maximum solutions depending on how tiresome your noise is (don't guess; only your neighbour will be able to say). The very least you can do is simply not use a room with a party wall, or transfer the guilty machine to the other end of the room. The next step up is to trace and block air leaks through the wall, which will be carrying noise as well. Make sure brick walls are well pointed and plastered from ceiling space to floor space – hoick out the skirting boards and make sure the plaster goes right down. If noise from an upper-storey room seems to be travelling upwards and then through the party wall in the loft, render or plaster that too.

The next stage is to discover whether or not the wall has a cavity. If it has, you should fill it as for thermal insulation: it might just be enough to tip the scales (in general, anything you do to improve thermal insulation will also have an effect on noise insulation, but not nearly to the same extent). If it has not got cavity insulation, or if filling it is not likely to do the trick, you will have to start thinking of maximum solutions involving structural alterations.

The first principle of noise insulation is that it increases with mass. However, it has been found that double-leaf walls provide noise insulation disproportionate to their combined mass – in other words, the space in between is helping. The wider this space is the better, and the same goes for the density of each leaf. Filling the space with sound-absorbent material like thermal insulating blanket or foam also helps. But any structural link between the two leaves diminishes the effect enormously.

The easiest way to achieve this double leaf is to take up the floorboards near the wall and cut back the ceiling as far as you can spare the space (at least 75mm). After inspecting your side of the party wall for air passages, as described above, suspend insulating blanket of a thickness equal to the amount you have cut back the ceiling, then support it against the existing wall with a framework of timber anchored to the floor and ceiling joists. This in turn will support a new inside wall of plasterboard, which should have two layers, the second overlapping the joins of the first.

The important feature of this construction is that there is no structural link between the new wall and the old – just absorbent material pressed between them. If there has to be a link for any reason, the insulation achieved may not be worth the cost, but you could minimise transmission through the link by padding both ends with rubber or some such resilient material.

This type of insulation should be capable of suppressing noise from even the most sophisticated home workshop, but if you are in doubt as to its effectiveness, don't try it – this is an area in which trial and error can be expensive. The ultimate solution, short of rebuilding your whole house, is to build a concrete wall from the floor space to the ceiling space, 250mm back from the original wall. This should do the trick on its own, but absorbent material in the cavity would not be wasted. This is, of course, an expensive

and quite complicated business and reduces the room space considerably, especially if you are forced to do it on every wall.

The same basic principles apply to ceilings and floors; a 'floating floor' mounted on structural foam provides good noise insulation, for instance. The minimum solutions are simply to seal gaps, fill spaces beneath floorboards with absorbent material and lay hardboard, underlay and thick carpet on the floor of the room above.

Doors and windows present special problems. Windows should be double glazed with the panes at least 125mm apart for effective noise insulation, and at least one of the panes should have a resilient mounting. Heavy, pressure-sealed double doors would be best, but a small lobby can be quite effective, especially if it has absorbent material inside, even if this is only the family's hats and coats. At the worst, back the door with chipboard. Thorough draught-proofing should, of course, accompany all these methods, and a sound-proof mechanical ventilator may be needed.

Even if you have eliminated airborne sound effectively, it may still be transmitted indirectly through structures, and there is virtually nothing that can be done to counter this. However, vibration can be damped by mounting machines on resilient pads; and they should be on solid floors.

Acoustic tiles and materials for which natural noise insulation is claimed (like cork) can improve the acoustics inside a room – but they do little or nothing to prevent noise escaping. Since the purpose of noise insulation is to confine noise to the room in which it occurs, a well insulated room is likely to reverberate unpleasantly. It is at this point that sound-absorbent finishes for walls, floor and ceiling come into their own.

Safety

Safety is, or should be, a matter of simple common sense, but judging by accident statistics this is a quality in shorter supply than it should be. So here is a basic run-through of safety factors specifically related to leisure activities. Where appropriate, more detailed notes appear in individual sections.

The simplest precautions against accidents are good light and a clear head. Don't use tools or machinery when you are tired. Make sure that the general level of lighting is adequate and that machines are independently lit. Don't have strong contrasts between general and local lighting, or you could blur at a critical moment. Is the room warm enough? Cold hands are less safe than warm ones.

Fire

You should have a dry-powder fire extinguisher handy if you are using electrical appliances, and a bucket of sand or a fire blanket as an extra safeguard. Find out how to use the extinguisher before it is put to the test, and keep it really close to the working area, not somewhere across the room.

Avoid open fires altogether if you are using inflammable materials; open gas fires and electric radiant bars are best avoided too if small inflammable particles or dust are going to be flying about. If you use a gas burner or butane torch for heating materials, keep this area distinct from storage areas and keep odd rags or cotton waste under control. An electric ring would be safer than a gas one anyway. See the section on workshops in Part Three for special precautions when welding. Store all inflammable materials, especially chemicals, in a cool place.

Electricity

Quite low voltages can deliver a nasty shock, so treat all appliances with respect. Make sure everything is earthed unless it has double insulation (assume it hasn't unless the makers specifically say so). Check all flexes periodically for wear and replace immediately if you see any that are worn. Keep flexes as short as you can by installing power points close to where appliances are being used, but if they have to be run to distant points, make sure they do so where they cannot catch feet or equipment. Avoid multi-adaptors. In areas where liquids are used, always have pull-cords installed instead of switches, for appliances as well as lights.

Check that all appliances are switched off before you leave the room, even for just a minute or two, unless you lock the door behind you. Always ensure that 'off' switches break the live lead. For extra safety and convenience use sockets fitted with warning lights to tell you when an appliance is on. Watch out for power cuts, especially in relation to tools like soldering irons where it is not obvious whether they are on or off. Try and keep power points away from obvious conductors like metal pipes, radiators, and sinks. Moulded rubber plugs are less brittle than plastic ones, and hence less likely to break if hit.

Clothing

A pair of cheap PVC goggles should be worn whenever dust or particles fly, and face masks may be necessary when some woods or plastics are being worked. Special equipment is necessary when molten metal is in use and for welding (see section on workshops). Long hair should be tied up or netted when machines are in use, and stout shoes worn to guard against tripping. Avoid loose clothing, especially ties, when using rotary machines that you bend over, like lathes or buffing wheels.

Flameproof and sometimes chemical-resistant overalls are required in certain situations, and some kind of overall should be worn in workshops out of habit. Check that belts and apron strings are fastened tightly. If you are using a lot of synthetic materials check the advisability of using barrier creams and gloves.

Equipment

Where special precautions are needed with particular pieces of equipment, they are covered in individual sections in Parts Two and Three. In general, watch out for sharp edges, especially on cutting tools. Make sure saws, chisels, knives and so on are stowed away immediately after use, even if they will be needed again later.

Watch out for moving parts that might trap or burn skin or clothing. Watch out for emissions of heat, sparks, dust, particles and fumes. If you are really in command of equipment it should be second nature to anticipate potential sources of danger and take appropriate evasive action beforehand. Above all, keep your equipment in good condition and have machines regularly serviced.

Children

Ideally, children should be excluded altogether from a room where machines, tools, inflammable or toxic substances, heavy materials and electric appliances are kept. If that is too much to hope for, the next best thing is to see that all of these are kept out of reach. Electrical sockets and switches should be mounted at high level, and the advisability of warning lights is greater when children are around.

The other possible area of hazard for children is where space is limited as a result of structural alterations. Children should be kept away from narrow spiral stairs and especially from telescopic ladders into lofts – which is tantamount to saying these things are unsuitable for houses with young children.

First aid

A first-aid box should be kept in most leisure rooms. Don't tuck it away in the hope that you'll remember where it is when the time comes; keep it in the open and clearly marked. It should include a pair of blunt-ended scissors, a few bandages of different sizes including a triangular one for slings, sterilised cotton wool, adhesive plasters and strapping, some sterilised gauze for dressings, a mild antiseptic and some safety pins. Some specific additions may be necessary for particular risks, but don't amass huge amounts of esoteric medications – they're just confusing. A book on first aid, or attendance at a beginner's course, are recommended for people using workshops and other members of their families. Posters and instruction charts on the workshop wall are a useful precaution.

Notes for the disabled

Some of the activities this book covers will be beyond the capabilities of most disabled people, but others will be well within their scope. A British Standard Code of Practice gives comprehensive details of provision within the home for the disabled. Only the most basic points are covered here.

Layout

Working areas should be grouped round the walls in a logical manner reflecting the sequence of operations in a particular activity. This is at once to minimise the amount of movement required within the room, and to maximise the space available for it – especially important for people in wheelchairs.

Furniture

Working heights for both the ambulant and wheelchair disabled should be calculated in relation to elbow height in just the same way as that described in the section on working surfaces, but remembering that there may be a need for a horizontal grab-bar on the front of the worktop (for the ambulant), and that there must be room for the wheelchair to slide beneath the worktop (for wheelchair users).

Door handles, horizontal rails within the room, switches and controls for lights, heaters, ventilation and fire alarms should be a maximum of 1050mm from the floor. Vertical or horizontal grab-rails should be not more than 30mm in diameter. Electric sockets should be not lower than 450mm from the ground, with projecting rather than recessed toggles. A wall-mounted telephone should not be more than 900mm from the floor.

Storage

Shelves should ideally be between 700–1450mm off the floor for the ambulant, and 450–1100mm for those in wheelchairs, though these figures could rise to maxima of 1500mm and 1150mm respectively. Wheelchair users will be able to reach less far back on high shelves if there is an obstruction such as a worktop lower down.

Fixed cupboards and drawers closer than about 250mm to a corner are hard for wheelchair users to get at. Cupboard doors should be at least 1370mm from the nearest obstruction opposite.

Sinks

Sinks for wheelchair users should be slightly shallower than for other people – a maximum 130mm deep as against 150mm for the ambulant disabled. The rim of the sink should be 25mm beneath the elbow height of the ambulant, but sink height for wheelchair users should be tailored to the height of their wheelchairs, which must have clearance beneath – a height of about 650mm is usual, measured from the floor to the base of the bowl. Make sure all hot pipes are shielded, as people with paralysed legs will be unable to feel burns.

Floors and doors

Floor surfaces should be smooth and non-slip, without rugs and avoiding split levels. Doors should have a clear opening of at least 800mm, with an unobstructed area inside (on the latch side of the door) of another 380mm for wheelchair users. Latched doors should have levers rather than knobs, and have spring closures adjusted to a maximum tension of 7·5 kilogrammes per metre for internal doors, 13·5 kg/m for external.

Ramps up to outside doors should rise at maximum gradient of 1 in 12, be at least 220mm wide, and have 50mm kerbs on exposed sides. They should also have rails on both sides not more than 1050mm above the ramp itself.

Lighting

Good lighting is even more important for the disabled than for other users of leisure rooms. See section on lighting.

Heating

The disabled tend to need higher room temperatures. The recommendation for physically active areas is therefore a minimum 16°C and for sedentary areas a minimum 20°C. Heating should be kept low down. Underfloor heating is ideal, since it does not make the head hotter than the feet, but skirting heaters spaced around the room are an acceptable alternative. Radiators and hot pipes should be guarded to avoid burns. Free-standing electric and paraffin heaters should be avoided, as should open fires.

Safety

The points to watch out for, and the precautions to take, are not different in kind from those described in the last section. But extra care is needed when planning for the disabled, bearing in mind particularly that they are incapable of taking evasive action at the same speed as other people if accidents do happen.

Part Two
Clean hobbies

Writing

Of all hobbies, writing is probably the one that requires the least specialised attention. In fact, unless you intend to be professional about it, it's hardly worth a room to itself at all. But if you are doubling up, choose something like a bedroom where the second use will not intrude on the hobby. It should be as far from living areas as possible, to preserve your concentration and avoid inflicting typewriter noise on the rest of the family.

Layout

Where you are doubling up, the primary purpose of the room will largely dictate how you lay out the writing area. How you plan a whole writing room depends very much on personal taste. If it is small, the centre should be kept as free as possible, with working areas and storage distributed around the walls.

Relate functional areas if you can – if you have two worktops, for instance (one for longhand and reading, one for typing – see below) they could be at right angles and served by the same swivel chair. Working surfaces should be close to the window but a typing surface should not face the window unless there is good side light (such as in a bay window), or you will probably find the keyboard is either shadowed by the superstructure or reflects glare.

Some people enjoy being momentarily distracted from their work by things happening outside the window or within the room; others prefer to shut off the outside world by facing an austere blank wall when they work.

Furniture

The minimum requirements are a table and a chair. The table should be at elbow height for longhand writing and reading, but about 100mm lower for typing. If you have to compromise, do so on the lower height unless typing will be strictly occasional. Preferably, use two different surfaces for the two activities. Letting a well into the worktop is an alternative, but it is rather cumbersome and unsuitable for a portable typewriter as it will trap the carriage.

A typing worktop should be really solid, especially if an electric typewriter is being used – apparently robust tables all too often turn to jelly when you press the carriage return key. Desks designed for office use, often with steel frames, are excellent and usually incorporate either single or double, suspended or pedestal, drawer units. Modern office furniture can be quite attractive enough for the home. The desk surface should be non-slip; highly polished or plastic laminate surfaces are not advised.

The seat should simply be comfortable, and chosen in relation to the table to give correct support where it is needed (see section on working surfaces in Part One). Lumbar support is particularly vital, or you will quickly contract 'writer's back'. Typists' chairs are designed specifically for the purpose, and modern ones are a distinct aesthetic improvement on older versions. Those that have adjustable height can get over the disparity between typing and longhand writing heights, and allow the desk to be used comfortably by different people (if that's desirable).

Storage

You are bound to want some storage for papers, books and smaller tools like pens, paper clips, erasers and so on. A complete wall of books is not only tidy but it provides some noise damping, so choose the wall where this is most likely to be appreciated. Use a system of adjustable brackets so that outsize books can be accommodated.

Fitted filing drawers are generally an option with office desks, and this is a tidy way to store folders and loose papers, though box files on shelves will do. Moulded plastic trays are available for smaller items, and can sit on desk tops or in shallow drawers. If sterner filing is called for, filing cabinets or cupboards are the answer. These last can look remarkably like wardrobes when made in wood, and can be quite easily converted for this purpose if you want to integrate the two halves of a study/bedroom.

All these things can be duplicated at much less cost, but at some loss in aesthetics. You can, for instance, produce a serviceable desk by buying two low second-hand chests of drawers, stripping them down or just painting them, and bridging the gap between them with a plank of equivalent width. Old grey filing cabinets are widely available in junk shops, and take on a new lease of life if brightly painted; so do 'civil service' metal shelf units when similarly improved.

Below: a wall of bookshelves, with shallow drawers underneath the worktop and a sensible choice of chair.

Above: this well lit worktop is strengthened by tubular supports and covers a filing cabinet and a painted chest of drawers.

Lighting
Fluorescent tubes may seem a little clinical as the general lighting in a writing room, especially if it's doubling as something else; a well diffused tungsten source might be a better choice. Local lighting will be needed for the worktop and anywhere else the logic of use dictates. Adjustable table lamps are more versatile than spots; the choice depends on how much you anticipate adjusting them.

Heating
Writing is a very sedentary activity and will need as much heat as your living room – probably around 20–22°C. If this is not available from central heating, you will need a fast-response heater of at least 2kW and probably 3kW output. Make sure it has thermostatic controls if you don't want to be constantly interrupting your work to adjust it.

Walls and floors
Virtually any wall or floor covering is suitable, though some people will object to bold patterns. A good-sized pinboard either above or near the worktop is useful, but if unsealed cork tiles are chosen as the wall finish (good acoustics and some thermal insulation) they can do on their own if not punished too hard.

This music room has several good features, including well insulated walls, double-glazed windows and built-in storage for instruments, music, records and an audio system.

Music

Nothing can be calculated to annoy a neighbour more readily than a musical phrase or scale endlessly repeated, preferably on a trumpet. So at the outset it should be said that anyone planning a room for music practice, home recording, or just loud stereophony should read the section on noise in Part One very carefully. A room structurally detached from any other building, and purpose-designed for noise insulation, is the ideal.

Acoustics

Classically, a music room should have opposite walls at least seven degrees off parallel and a volume of irregular proportions like 1:2:3 or 3:4:5. This works out at a very odd shape indeed, however, and can only be managed in the sort of purpose-built outhouse mentioned above.

The next best thing is to avoid a square room, and go for a fairly high ceiling. Strategic use of sound absorbent materials will achieve a pleasant balance between resonance and clarity. Start with plenty of hard surfaces and gradually add curtains and absorbent wall finishes until you strike the right compromise. Screens can be used for fine tuning.

Layout

This is difficult to plan owing to the awkward shapes of some instruments and the different numbers of performers who may be present at any one time. It only makes sense to locate the piano permanently – other instruments are relatively portable. The piano should not be surrounded by other instruments, and the room must be so arranged that the pianist will have a clear view of other players, especially if conducting.

Upright pianos are around 1525mm long by 600mm wide, and are usually backed on to a wall. Grands have about the same length keyboard, but can be anything up to 2750mm wide. With a grand – which may have to be built into the room – the player often sits between the keyboard and a wall, in which case a good 900mm should be allowed for access.

Storage

There may be no need to store instruments other than the piano in the music room if players take their own away. Even if storage space is desirable, there might not be room for bulkier instruments like double basses (which measure, when cased, around $905 \times 685 \times 460$mm). If you want to, and can, accommodate instruments, careful design of cupboards will be necessary. The Department of Education and Science give a table of instrument sizes in their *Building Bulletin 30* (*Drama and Music*). The cupboards should have adjustable shelves that can be juggled to accommodate changes in the structure of your ensemble. Sliding doors can overcome the problem of access when the room is full.

A storage wall should also include space for sheet music and scores. Conventional filing cabinets or cupboards may be adequate, but some scores are very bulky. Although sheet music is traditionally stored flat, this entails a lot of rummaging. Experts say scores and sheets are better stood upright on shelves, in boxes with spring clips, labelled with composers' names or however you want to classify the music. Nearly all scores will fit into boxes 356×254mm.

Shelves 350mm high will accommodate all records, including boxed sets. If records (especially 78 rpm records, if you have any) are stood on open shelves, rigid dividers should be incorporated regularly along the length of the shelf to prevent too much weight pressing on the bottom record if they lean. A variety of proprietary record cases can be bought – their advantage is that they keep out dust better than open shelves.

Lighting

Windows should face north if possible, to avoid direct sunlight striking the instruments. Failing that, use adjustable louvre or pinoleum blinds to deflect the rays and keep down solar heating of the room. Good glare-free artificial lighting is required; this will probably have to be confined to general lighting, as providing local lighting for each player would be highly complicated and inflexible.

Heating

Musical instruments must be kept dry and as far as possible at a constant temperature. If they are to be stored in a room which is not itself kept heated, the storage cupboard should have its own heater like an airing cupboard and air should circulate well inside – helped by using slats instead of solid shelves. Special 40W heaters can be fitted to pianos. For general heating when the room is in use flexibility is called for as the amount of heat needed will vary with the number of the players present and, to some extent, with the tempo of the session.

Furniture

Almost every player has to sit, but postures vary widely from instrument to instrument. Seating should therefore not be shaped to body contours, and chairbacks are redundant – so stools are the best bet. Avoid moulded plastic fold-up or stackable chairs. A long mirror in which beginners can check their postures can be useful.

Dressmaking

This section is about a room for quite ambitious needlework, but much of it is relevant to a simpler household sewing room. Equally the suggestions can be adapted for part of a room, rather than a whole room – sewing can quite easily double with a spare bedroom.

There are no essential criteria involved in choosing a room for dressmaking, but if your house has thin walls, try to avoid a party wall and keep away from living areas, especially if you have an older (and hence louder) sewing machine.

Layout
The general sequence of operations is cutting out, machining, and pressing, so it makes sense to plan your working surfaces in that order. It is a good idea to group them on one wall, or running round a corner, so that a fair amount of floor area is left for dummies which you will want to be able to walk round freely and draw back from too.

Furniture
You need a really generous working surface for setting out, marking and cutting – at least 1800mm long and 900mm wide if you can manage it. If you have a large room, you might prefer to be able to walk all round this, but most people will use space better by placing it against a wall (where it is also safer if you lean on it for extra reach). The cutting table should be at elbow height for either a standing or sitting posture, according to your preference. If you are likely to do both, make it the standing height and get an adjustable typists' chair or a high stool for when you want to sit down.

You also need a generous surface area for the sewing machine, at least at the working end. Ideally this should be separate from the cutting table so you don't have to move all the pieces off when you start sewing – especially if you are doing more than one job at a time. But if space forces it, the cutting table could be used. The working height of the sewing machine may then be raised above elbow height, but an adjustable chair, or a stool related to the height of the machine rather than that of the table, will get over that. The ideal height for the sewing table is 100mm beneath the elbows.

Pressing must be done on a firm worktop – firmer than that customarily provided by portable ironing boards. The cutting table will not do, as a good pressing table must have a 'nose'. It should also stand 200mm below elbow height so that pressure can be applied to the iron. Ideally the pressing table should be almost as long as the cutting table, but this may be too much to hope for. If space is really tight, you will have no choice but to use a fold-up ironing board, either the portable kind or one built into a cupboard.

Storage
You need small-scale storage for pins, needles, reels, wool, material remnants and so on; also large-scale storage for hanging work in progress, storing dummies, perhaps the ironing board and the sewing machine, longer lengths of material etc.

A fitted drawer, or a shallow drawer with a moulded plastic tray, can hold pins, needles, crochet hooks and similar tools. Pegboard is suitable for larger tools like scissors, and for hanging reels of cotton in colour progression. Patterns, in their envelopes, are best kept in a drawer too. Fixed dividers along its length should keep order, allowing two or more rows to stand on their sides or ends. A lower drawer can be used for remnants.

A double wardrobe is the best answer to much of the larger-scale storage. One half should have a rail and hangers for work in progress and the other should have unimpeded space for storing dummies, the ironing board and rolls of material. If these are fitted wardrobes, there will almost certainly be shelf space at the top which can be used for a head block (if making hats), hat boxes, and other less frequently used objects.

It is likely that a little open shelf space will still be needed for things like bottles of cleaning fluid, the iron, and so on. Storing the sewing machine is a special problem. The portability of many machines is strictly theoretical, and you want to avoid lugging it around. If you can't have it standing out permanently, try and find space for a shelf at the same height as the sewing table, and as close to it as possible to minimise lifting. Some modern machines can be up-ended, which makes suitable storage space easier to find.

Lighting
You need good daylight, especially for cutting out and sewing. It is best to locate the cutting table under a window, as there will be nothing to cast shadows on the work. The sewing table, if separate, will be better sideways on to the window (the working end of the machine towards it), or the controls will be shadowed. Good artificial light is necessary, too – a mix of fluorescent tubes and spots is probably the simplest solution. If colour matching is important, choose the fluorescents with care – see the lighting section in Part One.

Heating
A room temperature between 18° and 22°C is required, but remember that the iron will generate a surprising amount of local heat. If you are using central heating or something else not readily adjustable, you will just have to accept this as an

For ambitious needlework you will need large, separate work surfaces for marking out and cutting, for sewing, and for pressing. Good daylight can be supplemented by a mixture of fluorescent lights and spotlights.

RICHARD DRAPER

occupational hazard. Otherwise choose a thermostatically controlled source which will shut itself off when the room over-heats. If your worktop faces a window, you may get too hot at certain times of day (depending on the direction the window faces), which you can combat by fitting louvre or pinoleum blinds. Vertical louvres catch dust less easily than horizontal ones. Remember that the room must be kept dry at all times to prevent equipment rusting.

Walls and floors

Sealed floorboards, cork or vinyl tiles and similar hard floor coverings are marginally easier to keep clear of bits of thread than carpet, but it's not worth making a fuss about it. Any wall finish at all will do; you may find it helpful to have a pin-up board somewhere in the working area.

Safety

No alarming revelations here – but be careful with the iron, which can easily be left on by mistake, especially if there's a power cut. If you do not have a purpose-made ironing board, get a piece of asbestos to stand the iron on, generous enough so that the face of the iron will fall on it if knocked over. Avoid trailing flexes where possible.

This small sewing room has been built into an alcove, with a door to hide it when not in use. The sewing table hinges down from the back wall and scraps of fabric are kept in the pockets on the back of the door.

Leatherwork

Leather crafts like glove-making and bag-making are rather robust variants of needlework, and the leatherworker's room will look like a cross between the dressmaking room just described and a small workshop. In fact this section should be read as a supplement to the last one.

Furniture
If you expect to try your hand at leather clothing, you will need a cutting table of the same dimensions as for dressmaking, but if you are sticking to bags, belts and bookmarks a much narrower table is sufficient (maximum 400mm wide), though the longer the better for belts. It could double as the work table if you are only working on one piece at a time, but otherwise you will find it more convenient to treat cutting and working as separate activities. Clothes apart, a leatherworker's room can be much smaller than a dressmaker's. Firm work tables and smaller cutting tables can be improvised from junk-shop furniture – you'll need your money for leather.

Storage
In addition to the suggestions in the last section, pegboard is a useful way of keeping the bulkier tools used in leatherwork – such as punching pliers. Transparent plastic boxes or old jam jars are ideal for small rivets, eyelets, buckles and studs. Leather skins should be rolled up and kept in boxes, or wrapped in paper (not plastic) and shelved.

Floors
Very small pieces of waste leather like punchings and shavings are rather difficult to extract from carpet; therefore an easily-swept hard floor covering like sealed cork tiles or vinyl might be better.

Lighting
Pay special attention to local lighting at the cutting table – the markings on leather can be hard to follow.

Toymaking

All the essential requirements of a soft-toy maker's room are the same as for the dressmaking room already described, except that the storage requirements are less, and there is no need for dummies; so a much smaller room, or part of a room, will be fine.

Furniture
The cutting table can be a lot more modest than for dressmaking; 900 × 500mm should be enough for the largest teddy bear. Again, it can double as the sewing table if need be, but remember that you have to have space for both the sewing machine and stuffing – so a separate worktop may be more useful.

Storage
There is no need for the large-scale storage described under dressmaking. Well spaced shelves are the best thing for completed toys and work in progress, and they are also decorative. Think carefully about storage for stuffing materials. The sort of half-moon frames some people use to support paper or plastic bags instead of dustbins might be a good idea – they can be either free-standing, or screwed to the end of the sewing table for easy reach. Transparent bags make it easy to see when you need to re-stock.

Floors
Some stuffing materials have a peculiarly tenacious grip on carpet and other soft furnishings (also clothes!) – latex scraps are particularly bad in this respect. Sealed cork tiles, vinyl or plain floorboards (sanded and sealed) would be easier to keep clean.

A floor loom like this takes up a lot of space, but if you're tidy there's no reason for it to be locked away in a room of its own. A spinning-wheel might be fitted in as well, but dyeing should be kept to a separate area.

SPIKE POWELL/ELIZABETH WHITING

Weaving and spinning

Weaving – like fishing – is almost a way of
life. There is something mysterious about
it that binds its devotees in a sort of
unofficial freemasonry. Although to the
non-initiate it seems as complex as
calculus, its requirements in terms of
space, storage and furniture are
surprisingly straightforward.

You can weave almost anywhere big
enough to take the loom, and where table
looms are concerned this is not at all a
demanding condition. However, most
learner-weavers aim to graduate eventually to a foot-operated floor loom, so you
should plan for expansion when you
choose your weaving room. In fact a well
looked after loom is not an eyesore in a
lounge or some similar room if you have a
space problem.

The need for space grows more pressing
if, as most weavers do at some point, you
intend to try your hand at spinning. Of
course, hand-spinning or using a simple
spindle does not take up much room, but
if you are going to mass-produce home-
spun you will almost certainly need a
spinning wheel.

At a third level of involvement, you
may want to do your own dyeing, in which
case still more space is needed for a dyebath and a drying area – both well out of
splashing range of the wheel and the loom.
By this time a dual-purpose room is
virtually out of the question. If you are
likely to get involved in dyeing (almost
inevitable at some point if you are
spinning a lot of your own wool), the
availability of water becomes an important
consideration.

Layout

It is hard to generalise about this – it will vary so much with your level of expertise and the shape of the room. Taking the maximum situation, you will have three distinct zones of activity – spinning, dyeing and weaving. The importance of keeping dyeing well away from the other two has already been noted. You will probably want to have access to both the spinning wheel and a floor loom from all sides, in case of tangles, so they will have to stand free wherever space allows. If, as seems sensible, you back the seat on to a wall in both cases, make sure you leave at least 900mm for access.

Table looms take up much less space, but this (apart from their cheapness) is the only advantage they have over foot looms for the experienced weaver. The worktop on which they are placed should not face a window, as the heddles and their frame will cast confusing shadows. This does not apply, of course, to flat tapestry and board looms.

Furniture

Strictly speaking the worktop for a table loom need be only fractionally larger than the loom itself – a likely maximum of 1000 × 600mm. But remember that you will be sitting at the end, not the side, of this area. If you do not have shelves within reach for spare bobbins, reference books and so on, you may prefer to have a wider table to accommodate some of these beside the loom. The height of the actual working surface will be about 100mm above the worktop, which should be reduced from elbow height accordingly. If you are graduating from a table to a floor loom, you may feel that it makes sense to dispense with the worktop to make more space. However, don't do this unless you are sure you will not want somewhere to draw up patterns on squared paper before weaving : many weavers do.

Remember that the working surface on a floor loom is the height of the cloth beam; you should choose, or modify, your seat so that this is at elbow height. On the spinning wheel, the spinning head should be at elbow height when you are seated.

If you are dyeing your own wool, you will need a sink, a dyebath (either on a gas or electric burner, or a clothes boiler, depending on the volume you dye at a time) and an adjoining worktop for preparing dyes and standing the burners or boiler. Worktop height here should be 100mm below the elbow, too, and although the sink rim should strictly be higher than this, it would be better to fit it flush with the worktop considering that you will be moving heavy dyebaths and saturated wool around.

It would be a good idea to keep one end of the worktop as a 'clean' zone where wool is prepared for dyeing, and the other end (or a drainer to the sink) as a 'dirty' zone for preparing dyes, using the burner or boiler to divide the two. Even so, care must be taken to avoid splashing dye on undyed materials.

Storage

The weaving and spinning areas both need a limited amount of shelf storage for odd bobbins, thread hooks, 'lazy kates', skein winders, reference books and such-like. In both cases this kind of storage should be accessible to one hand or the other without leaving the seat – which probably means using free-standing bookcases rather than wall-mounted shelves.

More shelf space is needed at the dyeing worktop, preferably immediately above it and extending as far as the sink, so that dye containers and anything else potentially contaminating can be kept clear of raw wool at the 'clean' end of the worktop. Scoured or dyed wool will drip as it dries, so the skeins should be hung from wall-mounted bars (such as those often found in kitchens for tea-towels) either above the sink or, if that is inconvenient, over a special drainage area let into the floor.

Drawing paper is best stored flat in drawers under a worktop, but if this is impossible, store it rolled in cardboard or plastic tubes – offcuts of PVC rainwater pipe from a builders' merchant would do fine. These could be racked horizontally or vertically. But if there is any need for storage of finished articles (if you are weaving for Christmas, or commercially) a chest of shallow drawers might be worth the investment.

Lighting
Good daylight is best, and the direction of light may be a major factor in deciding the layout of the room. Watch out for inadvertent shadowing by the rather intricately shaped parts of looms and spinning wheels. It would be wise to sort this out by trial and error before planning the location of fixed shelving and worktops. Good general lighting is needed at night, with local light above the loom,

the wheel and the worktops. Well shaded, suspended tungsten lights will probably be better than spots for the loom and the spinning wheel. A pull-cord should be used for the light above the scouring/dyeing area.

Heating
Weaving can be slow and relaxing or fast and energetic according to your mood, but it is a seated activity, as is spinning, and will need a fairly substantial level of heat: it could be anywhere between about 16° and 20°C. Clearly you need flexibility, and the best solution will probably be background heating (from central heating or night storage heaters) supplemented by some quick response system like fan heaters. Thermostatic controls are advisable to prevent breaks in concentration while you adjust them; this would also iron out temporary inconsistencies in room temperature caused by the boiler or burner during dyeing. Try to avoid too great a contrast between the heat of the room when you are working in it and the general background heat, for the sake of your wool.

Floors and walls
For weaving and spinning, almost any floor covering will do, including carpet, although it might be slightly easier to clean up small scraps of waste from a hard surface. Around the scouring/dyeing area, however, something scrubbable like vinyl is essential. Wall finish is inconsequential except around the sink and its adjoining worktop, where the finish should again be scrubbable – ceramic tiles, vinyl or sealed cork are recommended.

Part Three
Dirty hobbies

This is an ideal studio built for a professional painter, Richard Ewen, who lives in Wiltshire. Michael Pearson, the architect, has paid particular attention to lighting, with tall, north-facing windows, fluorescent strips and spotlights.

Painting

Painters are often rather disorganised people, and their studios tend to be an ergonomist's nightmare – old paint tubes, discarded props, half-finished paintings and junk-yard furniture scattered everywhere. There is a certain romantic appeal in this image, but if you're setting up a studio from scratch, a little forethought can save a lot of chaos. Life will be difficult enough in your struggling years without wantonly adding other problems.

Layout

The primary constraint in planning your room is that the main work surface – the easel – gets plenty of daylight. This will not be achieved if either it or you backs on to the window. The light should strike the easel either sideways or at some over-the-shoulder angle, provided that the window is high enough. Rooflights are better still, flooding the room with a fairly consistent light. You will want to stand well back from the picture, so the easel should stand in plenty of floor-space with no encumbrances through a wide angle in front of it. Other working surfaces should be spaced around the walls as space allows.

Furniture

You will need at least one long, but not too wide (400mm or so) worktop on which to keep materials in constant use. If you intend to stretch your own canvases, or do any framing, a wider table about 600–900mm wide which can be pulled into the centre of the room will be useful, but if space is tight, this can double as the general worktop.

The worktop itself will not be in use that much, or for long periods at a time, so its height is not critical – anything from elbow height to 100mm beneath will be comfortable. In general it is worth saving money by buying second-hand furniture for studios, as painting is one hobby where money must not be skimped on tools and materials. Under no circumstances should you assume that studio furniture will ever be usable for any other purpose, but if there is a reason to keep the worktop clean, either cover it with newspaper or use a laminated finish.

Despite the need to keep the easel area unencumbered, most painters like to have a small table about 400mm square a little below elbow height, set in front and to one side of the easel within convenient reach of their brush hand. This is for storing a selection of brushes, rags and paint tubes in use on the current picture. It is probably a good thing to have this table on castors, with lips around its edges to stop things falling off. If you find it distracting to turn your eyes off the work in progress, an alternative is to fit a shallow shelf just beneath the lower jaw of the easel.

Most painters do a lot of drawing, and you will probably want to keep an area of worktop reserved for this (using the general worktop is not a good idea, as the drawings will get paint-stained), or a free-standing drawing board. The lighting requirements for this are similar to those for the easel. It is possible to buy purpose-designed desks which have built-in drawing boards that fold down to form a flat surface, and if you are in need of an extra worktop, this could be useful.

Depending on how long you intend to remain in front of the easel at a stretch, you may like to have a stool nearby. It should be high enough so that the

A folding drawing board like this one by British Thornton is a useful accessory in most studios.

relationship between the painting and your head and hands is not greatly disturbed when you sit down. The same stool, or others, can also be used at the drawing board and worktop.

Storage

Some medium-sized shelves about 300–400mm wide are useful for props; adjustable ones provide greater flexibility for the future. If you use a lot of drapes in your subjects, an old chest of drawers is useful, and the top drawers can be used for smaller, more delicate pieces of equipment. On the whole, though, painters can't be bothered rummaging – they like to be able to lay their hands on things as soon as they are needed. A lot of basic equipment will therefore lie out on the worktop, including paint tubes and brushes (the latter should be stood, heads upward, in jam jars or the like).

The only real exception to the second-hand furniture rule might be specialised storage. If you are going to keep large sheets of drawing paper, wide shallow drawers are the best way to keep them flat. Special-purpose units can be bought from drawing office suppliers, but if you're a reasonable handyman you might be able to run up an equivalent yourself. A highly *ad hoc* alternative is to hang the paper from bulldog clips tied to the rail

of an old wardrobe (to keep out dust); or you could roll the paper and use off-cuts of PVC rainwater pipe from a builders' merchants to store it upright or slung in a rack under the worktop.

Finished paintings are best stored, facing inwards, against one wall, and it is a good idea to keep a whole wall free for this purpose. A series of battens at different distances from the wall should be fixed to the floor, to prevent slipping and to stop too much weight piling up. Smaller paintings should go at the bottom of the pile.

A professional drawing table and plan chest may be the answer if your hobby includes a lot of draughtsmanship. These models are from Magpie Furniture Ltd.

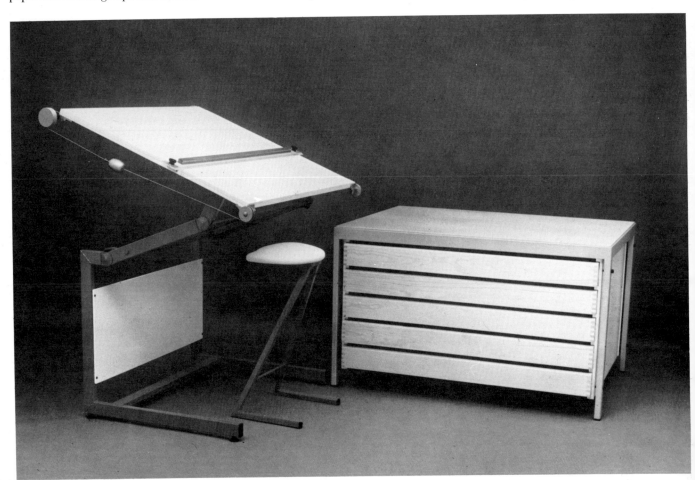

Lighting

A lot of daylight is needed in a studio, and the tips for making the most of what is available given in the section on lighting in Part One should be followed. It is fashionable nowadays to despise as Victorian the notion that this light should come from the north, but there is still a lot of sense in the old chestnut – north light is more consistent through the day, and it obviates direct sunlight which can overheat a room with a lot of glass. Daylight should also preferably come from up above, especially in cities and valleys where overshadowing is a problem.

Of course few of us have, or could afford to install, a huge plate-glass window canted at 45 degrees to the northern sky, but this is roughly what compromises should be aiming at. It can sometimes be achieved in attics, but bear in mind the strictures on cleaning; in single-storey buildings, rooflights are the best solution. In houses of two or more storeys, an upstairs room will usually be lighter than a downstairs one. Studio windows should occupy a lot of the wall into which they are set, and preferably be undivided sheets of glass with unobtrusive mountings.

Use fluorescent tubes set well above eye-level for basic artificial light, bearing in mind that they must be checked for colour accuracy (see section on lighting in Part One). These should be augmented by local lighting at the easel, worktop and drawing board. Spots are excellent in all these places, though some people might prefer the greater flexibility of an adjustable table lamp at the drawing board; it should be clamped on. Some painters like to bathe their subjects in floodlight; adjustable, free-standing photographers' floods are one possibility, or you can get flood attachments for a continuous power track, which can then take care of the spots as well.

Heating

The artistic temperament apart, painting is not a highly active occupation, so heating should be within the range recommended for sedentary activities. Cold hands are less sensitive than warm, remember. Canvases stretched in humid conditions will stay taut in dry atmospheres, but those stretched in dry rooms may sag slightly in humid ones. This is not a critical point, but it might be wise to hang a humidifier on a central heating radiator. On the other hand, varnishing has to be done in a very dry atmosphere to prevent 'blooming' and tools used for stretching canvases and making frames might rust in too humid an environment, so flexibility will be needed.

Walls and floors

Any hard floor covering is suitable for a studio, but usually it will be best to stick to light, neutral colours all round, with the ceiling white. Gloss paint is suitable for the walls, except immediately round the worktop where a tougher finish like vinyl tiles or ceramic tiles is easier to keep clean.

Safety

If you use gas or electric rings for heating size or varnish, make sure that inflammable materials (especially cotton rags) are kept away from the burners, and that the pan sits securely on the ring. Good ventilation is needed.

Varnish is a toxic substance which presents few dangers if painted on, but can be risky if sprayed. This is not likely in a home studio, but the solution is either to wear an industrial breathing mask (suitable for gases, not just dust) or to spray into a special varnishing booth fitted with an extractor.

Sculpture

The problem with modern sculpture is that it is so diverse. Materials commonly used include stone, metal, wood, plastics, clay, ivory, brick – even soap! As a result, the studios of professional sculptors specialising in different materials have very little in common. The metal sculptor's studio, for instance, will look more like a metal workshop than the room of a fellow-sculptor working in stone.

However, this book is not for professionals, and the assumption behind this section is that there is a demand for a general-purpose sculpture studio capable of housing experiments in a variety of materials. Even so, a lot of the detailed requirements are identical to those in other sections, so apologies in advance for multiple cross-references.

Location

The weight of the material you use, or intend using in the future, is a constraint that governs a lot to do with the design of your studio. Large lumps of stone or similar materials may dictate a room with a solid floor, and one involving the least amount of transport – which means being on the ground floor, or (less suitable) in a basement. Availability of water is an important criterion. Other things being equal, choose the room with the best light (see opposite).

Layout

Again the weight consideration is important here. If you confine yourself to small pieces you will probably just use an ordinary worktop, turning the piece on a turntable rather than walking round it. This will save space and make lighting much less of a problem. In this case you should place the worktop so that it gets the maximum overhead, side or over-the-shoulder daylight consistent with your being able to stand well back from the piece and view it from side angles.

If the work is heavy or fragile, however, you will need to use a purpose-built banker placed in the centre of the room so that you have plenty of space to move round the piece and stand back from it at any point. Multi-angle lighting then becomes a problem.

Furniture

Again, the diversity of sculpture makes it difficult to generalise. It is a fact of sculpting life that you will have to endure uncomfortable working postures for some of the time, and the bigger the piece the less time you will spend working at a convenient height.

Don't despair altogether, though. The basic rule is that the piece you are working on should be at or below elbow height, and the general working surface 100mm beneath the elbows will cater for a fair number of smaller pieces. If you are doing highly intricate work, the level should be much nearer the eyes – between 100–300mm beneath. Rather than stoop, make a separate high-level working surface at one end of your worktop, or use a block or box to raise the piece to the right height.

The worktop itself, assuming for the moment that you are not using bankers, need be nothing special – a junk-shop kitchen table will do provided that it is sturdy. Block it up or stand it on a plinth if it is not high enough as bought. If you are using bankers, you may well find that you build up a collection at different heights. You may then want to use a purpose-designed modelling stand, so make sure it has a good range of height adjustment and is on castors. If large stone sculptures are your thing you might find it useful to have a low-level trolley on wheels for transporting the block; some sculptors never remove the block from the trolley at all, using it as a banker. If you do this, make sure you put wedges under the wheels when you work on it.

If you are clay modelling you will need a secondary worktop, which can again be a sturdy old table, with its surface about 100mm below elbow height. Clay can be stored in buckets with tight-fitting lids (you will probably need three – one for clay in use, one for clay which has become too dry, and one for clay which is being reconditioned after drying out completely; you simply rotate the buckets as you empty them). The sink should ideally be a special large casting sink, but if this is beyond your pocket try for the largest available second-hand kitchen sink. You will need a heavy-duty sludge trap.

Storage

Allow plenty of shelf space for work in progress, finished pieces, clay models, moulds, ancillary materials (polish, colouring agents, etc). In some cases there may be a need for shallow drawers to hold small tools, but plastic trays on shelves could be just as good.

Most tools can be hung on pegboard – an especially good solution if you are using a conventional worktop, as you can use the wall above the working surface. A tidy possibility if you are working round a banker is to build yourself a small A-section trolley and face both sides with pegboard so that the tools can be kept ready at hand.

If a damp cupboard is needed, see under storage in the section on pottery.

Lighting

This is no less important for sculptors than for painters, and the comments on daylight in the section on painting apply equally here. The direction from which the light comes is perhaps less important unless you are using colour, but the three-dimensional aspect of sculpture often poses a problem. Where feasible, flooding the room with daylight from rooflights is the best solution. Failing this, a large expanse of window complemented by gloss-painted walls in a light neutral tone is the nearest compromise. There may be a case for judiciously placed mirrors.

Good, high-level general artificial lighting is needed, too, and is best provided by fluorescents. Be careful about colour accuracy if you are using colour. Spots can be used to supplement fluorescents if you are sculpting on a worktop, but are unlikely to be appropriate for bankers. In fact, you may have to rely entirely on general lighting for larger pieces, in which case make sure it is strong enough to make up for the lack of local lighting.

Heating

Physical activity varies from material to material and sometimes from operation to operation, so flexibility is the important thing. Some background heat from a radiator or night-storage heater is useful, but keep it fairly low and supplement it when necessary with a fan heater or an electric bar, mounted high up on a wall out of harm's way.

Walls and floors

Broadly, as for painting. In some cases a floor that can be sluiced down is ideal – see the section on walls and floors in Part One. The drain will require a sludge trap. Sluicing apart, choose a tough finish that will take regular scrubbing.

Safety

Fine, inflammable dust is sometimes present in sculptors' studios, so good ventilation is needed. Fires with open flames should be avoided for the same reason. Pull-cords should be used instead of switches for electrical appliances in areas where the hands may be wet. Portable electric fires should not be used.

Sculptors use a lot of sharp tools, and care should be taken to replace them in their storage immediately after use, even if they will soon be needed again. It is especially important not to leave cutting tools lying around close to the work where they might get covered by dust or shavings. Power tools should not be left connected to a distant socket when they are not being used or someone will trip over the flex.

Special precautions are needed for sculpture involving welded metal – see under welding in the section on workshops.

Val Barry's basement pottery has an electric wheel and kiln, but no other expensive special equipment. Plenty of strong shelving and some sturdy tables are quite sufficient.

Pottery

A potter's studio needs a supply of cold water, and this is one factor which will loom large in the choice of room. Two less obvious ones should be borne in mind, however. If you anticipate graduating in the future to a high-capacity kiln, you may need a solid floor; and if you buy clay in bulk, you won't want to carry it very far. These two suggest a ground-floor or basement room.

In an ideal world, the kiln would in fact be housed in its own ante-room, which would be unheated and have extra-powerful ventilation. In practice, however, this is not likely to be possible except in the rare case of a purpose-designed outhouse.

Layout
The sequence of activities in a potter's studio is splendidly methodical, so layout presents few problems. Work areas should be against the walls to ensure ease of movement, and the room should be planned either clockwise or anti-clockwise in this order: clay storage, wedging, sink, throwing or modelling, decorating and moulding, glazing, firing.

Furniture
Horizontal worktops are required for wedging, decorating and moulding, and glazing. The wedging bench requires downward force, and should therefore be at least 200mm below elbow height. It should have a surface area of at least one square metre and be very strong and solid – at least 50mm thick. For extra security (it comes in for a lot of punishment) it should be anchored to the floor or wall.

The other two benches need not be so strong, or so big. They could be 900 × 600mm, with surfaces around 30mm thick. They should be 100mm below the elbows unless you are using a turntable in decorating, in which case its bench should be 200mm below.

These dimensions are only given as a guide, however. It is worth scouring junk-shops for really tough, old-fashioned kitchen or garden tables. These are about the right height for wedging, and possibly decorating. For the other operations they can be quite simply blocked up, or just stood on a plinth. Alternatively, you can reduce your own height by sitting at a high stool. The reason for skimping on furniture is simple – the kiln, which may cost £500 or more.

The sink needs only a cold water supply, though the availability of hot to take the chill off in winter would be a kindness. The plug-hole must be fitted with a sturdy clay trap. Taps should be 400mm above the bottom of the sink to allow for filling buckets.

Storage
Clay is usually kept in plastic dustbins, without removing it from the plastic sack in which it is bought. If you buy in bulk, it's a good idea to keep clay you are not using outside the studio in a dry, cool place. Prepared slip and glaze should be kept in buckets or similarly sized containers at the sides of the decorating and glazing tables respectively (right-hand side for right-handed potters). These must have fitted lids and should be clearly labelled. Using one colour of bucket for slip and another for glaze (you will normally have more than one bucket of each around at a time) helps to prevent confusion.

Generous shelf space should be provided close to the wheel for thrown pots, and near the kiln for drying and completed pieces. In a small-scale studio, adjustable cantilevered shelves about 150mm wide are adequate, but a larger operation will probably need longer and wider, floor-standing, units with slatted shelves for drying pots at the kiln end. It is common practice for potters to place completed pots on a plank (about 900 × 150mm) as they come off the wheel, and then slide full planks on and off shelves and worktops until the pots are ready to be fired.

A 'damp cupboard' may be necessary to store work in progress; custom-built damp cupboards are lined with zinc and have sealable doors. However, a rough-and-ready damp cupboard can be made by covering the shelves of an old cupboard with zinc and laying a layer of plaster over the floor. Make sure the damp cupboard is clear of hot pipes and radiators, and as far away as possible from the kiln. In extremity you can simply cover pots with polythene bags, but you run the risk that the subsequent condensation will soften them.

If you are using moulds, they can be stored on vacant shelf space, or under worktops. Raw plaster should be kept dry, in a wood or metal container. Plaster and clay must never be allowed to mix. Plastic trays are useful for small tools, rulers and wire. Alternatively, use drawers slung under worktops.

Lighting

Good daylight should be available, preferably through rooflights in a single-storey building. Artificial light should include good general lighting and local lighting for each of the worktops, the wheel and possibly the kiln. Wall or ceiling-mounted spots are good in most cases, but at the decorating bench, where fine work is involved, the greater flexibility of an adjustable table lamp may be more suitable. If so, it should be clamped to the table, not stood on it.

Walls and floors

You should preferably be able to sluice your studio floor down to a central or side gutter and drain – see section on flooring in Part One. If so, make sure you have a clay trap over the drain. If sluicing is impossible, choose a tough waterproof surface that can be scrubbed well and often. The floor should be generously coved up the walls to a height of 200–300mm. Wall finishes should be waterproof (polyurethane gloss paint is a tough finish) with extra protection from ceramic tiles or vinyl round the sink and above worktops. Light colours will help reflect daylight round the room.

Heating

Activity in a potter's studio varies widely from the sedentary (decorating, glazing) to the downright aggressive (wedging), so heating has to be equally versatile. Thermostatic controls are good at coping with intermittent heating from the kiln, and a quick response is desirable at other times, all of which points to fan heaters. If they are mounted on a wall, they will not be tripped over. There is little point having any background heating – it will be redundant when the kiln is on and when you are not in the room.

Safety

A kiln can be a dangerous thing to anyone not accustomed to them. You should keep the door to the pottery locked at all times when you are not in it, and for belt-and-braces safety, have a separate lock on the kiln door so that it cannot be inadvertently opened when it is on. An isolating switch should be mounted on the wall at high level, out of reach of children. The same goes for an electrically operated wheel, except that pull-cords should be used instead of switches in any area where the hands will be wet.

Val Barry designed this wheel for her own use, but it could be easily copied and adjusted to suit other potters. It can be used either as a simple kick wheel or with a motor, as shown.

Photography

Describing the ideal room to make into a photographer's darkroom is a good deal easier than finding it. It should have a water supply (cold for black-and-white, hot and cold for colour), be windowless, dry and at a constant temperature, have double doors with a small lobby between, and have light-free ventilation to the outside of the house.

Unfortunately this precise combination is pretty rare, and you will almost certainly have to simulate some of these conditions and compromise on others. Setting up a really good darkroom can be expensive. But as any frustrated photographer who has fumed in the bathroom will confirm, it's money well spent.

Water

Providing water where it does not exist is likely to be the most expensive alteration – see the section on plumbing in Part One. Where possible use the existence of at least a cold water supply as your first criterion for choosing a room, but remember that it must be fed from the cold tank, not from the mains.

If you need to extend the plumbing, think carefully about whether you should save money now by making it a cold supply only, or save later expense by installing hot as well. This will depend on whether you intend graduating to colour in the future, or whether the room will at some point revert to some other use for which a hot and cold supply would be desirable.

Blackout

If the room has a window, it will have to be meticulously blacked out. You will need a special wooden frame fitted exactly to the dimensions of the window, and covered with black felt or velvet. If that has an expensive ring to it, use the felt or velvet round the edges only, and black paper over the rest of the area. The door will have to be sealed round the edges (metal strip draught excluder should be adequate), and if you are lucky enough to have double doors with a small lobby, seal both sets of doors and paint the lobby matt black all over. Either way, lock or bolt the inside door when you're working to stop anyone bursting in.

Effective light-proofing will make the room pretty airtight as well, so good ventilation is necessary. Mechanical ventilation that excludes light is best, but if that is too costly, the door or doors can be adapted to let in air but not light. With hollow core doors, this is done by drilling a row of holes at different heights in each skin; with solid doors, you will have to remove a panel and replace it with a tongue-and-groove section that allows air to pass up the groove on one side, over the tongue in the centre, and down the groove on the inside to enter the room.

Layout

There are distinct wet and dry processes, and the room should be divided to reflect this division. Thus the 'wet' side will contain the sink, the developer, the fixer and associated storage; on the 'dry' side you find the enlarger, paper storage, masking frame, glazing sheets, guillotine and dryer. If possible all working surfaces should be against walls, with associated storage above or below. Darkrooms lend themselves to long, narrow spaces where you don't have to keep crossing the room.

Furniture

All work areas except the sink require horizontal work surfaces, which should be at elbow level or not more than 100mm beneath. Theoretical exceptions to this are the enlarger (if it is table-mounted) and the guillotine, where the actual working surfaces would be somewhat higher than the surrounding worktop, but it will be a matter of personal choice whether the time spent at these machines justifies sinking them into wells. If the enlarger is wall-mounted, there may be a need for the worktop beneath to be adjustable in height to accommodate really large work. If it is table-mounted, the table must be very solid to prevent vibration.

One of the main working surfaces in the 'wet' area will be the bottom of the sink, which should be fitted with duck-boarding. The top of the duckboard should be about 800–850mm from the floor for a person of average height, with the sink sides 150–250mm high. The sink has to be special-purpose (ordinary sinks are not large enough); it is usually made out of solid wood, either lead-lined, un-lined or with a detachable plastics liner, or from bitumen-coated plywood. Taps should be at least 400mm above the bottom of the sink and, if colour work is tackled, a thermostatically controlled tap will be needed to ensure a constant temperature.

Storage
Use the space above and below the work-tops for storage. Shelves above should be used for chemicals, measuring jars, timer, books etc. Shallow drawers or shelves in cupboards beneath should be used for storing paper, prints and negatives. A light-proof drawer should be incorporated for open packets of sensitised materials.

If the room is too small to allow trays to stand out, vertical racks beneath the worktop will hold them. Cupboard space may be needed for mounting equipment, printing frames, photographic gear and the guillotine if it can't stand out. Drying negatives may be hung from a line, or from hooks set into the underside of high-level shelves, but some photographers prefer to hang them inside tall, ventilated cupboards (like changing-room lockers) to exclude dust.

Lighting
Lack of light is the important condition of a darkroom, but one or two 'safe lights' will be needed, and electric points should be provided for them. Portable safe lights are useful, but if they are fixed it is important that one illuminates the timer during developing. Other electric sockets will be needed for the enlarger and the dryer. General lighting is needed for non-sensitive operations – fluorescent tubes or a well diffused tungsten source are satisfactory. Since there is a lot of liquid about in darkrooms, you should use pull-cords rather than switches for all appliances.

Heating
Darkrooms should be kept fairly constant in temperature, but not too hot. A dark-room inside the shell of a centrally heated house may need no extra heat. Otherwise a light-free electric heater (such as an oil-filled radiator, but watch out for pilot lights) will be adequate when the room is in use. A fan heater can be used to boost the temperature provided that it can be turned off when sensitive materials are about; some mechanical ventilators designed for darkrooms incorporate heaters. It is important to keep a thermo-meter on the wall so you can be sure of developing at the same temperature each time; if you do not, you will find it almost impossible to achieve the same effect twice, except by accident!

Walls and floors
Walls and ceilings should all be painted white, preferably with the ceiling matt and the walls semi-gloss to reflect 'safe light'. A corrosion-resistant finish such as melamine or ceramic tiles should be used to protect the walls around the 'wet' area from chemical splashes. The floor, too, should be corrosion-resistant as well as waterproof and non-slip. Asphalt would be a good choice, or alternatively vinyl. The floor should be generously coved up the walls to about 200–300mm high. The wall finish around the enlarger should be matt black to prevent disturbing local reflections.

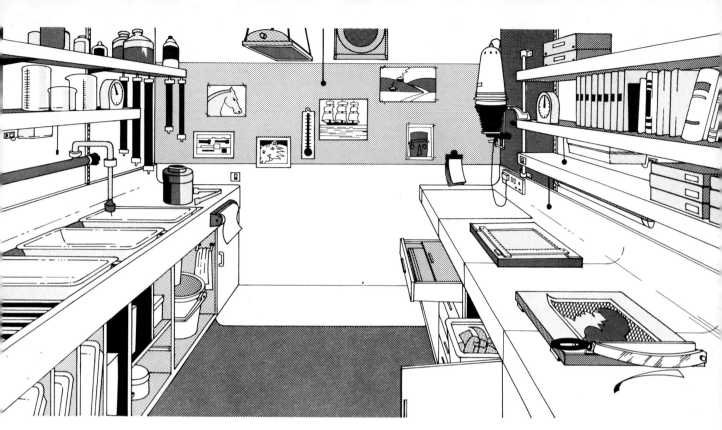

If possible, a photographic darkroom should have separate 'wet' (left) and 'dry' (right) areas, as here, with mechanical ventilation. Storage needs to be carefully planned to keep equipment clean and dust-free.

Jewellery

At its simplest, involving only a work-bench and some small-scale storage, jewellery is a hobby excellently suited to the home. Although it is classed here as a 'dirty' hobby (because it needs water and uses acid), it makes very little mess. Furthermore, although running water is needed, a capacious sink is not necessary; a bedroom basin would be adequate. So a home jeweller's workshop can combine very nicely with a room used for other purposes.

The only constraint apart from water supply is noise. Buffing wheels have an irritating sound, and so have tumble-polishers if you are trying your hand at lapidary work as well (also these go on 24 hours a day – very aggravating). Try to avoid party walls, and a certain amount of attention may have to be paid to sound insulation (see noise section in Part One).

Layout

A jeweller's bench can be very compact so there is virtually no layout problem. You will want a central working area with the annealing pan on one side and the buffing wheel on the other. If you want side light from a window, make sure the buffing wheel is on the other side, or you will be shadowed.

Furniture

The working area need be no bigger than around 1500 × 400mm, and since jewellery is usually small, the bench should be at elbow height for either a standing or sitting position (most jewellers sit). If you want to have both available, choose the standing height and use an adjustable chair with a footrest to provide seating when wanted. There will be occasions when you will want to work nearer to eye level, and the adjustable chair solution would cater for that, too. Or a block could be stood on the worktop to raise the height of the work.

Storage

The main need is to store small tools and pieces of material, and it is important to take care about this as a lot of jewellery materials are very expensive in relation to their bulk: untidiness could carry a financial penalty.

A lot of the tools (hammer, mallet, piercing saw, pliers) can be hung from pegboard immediately above the worktop, but some others (files, scriber, tweezers, burnisher) are best kept in a shallow drawer, either fitted or with a moulded plastic tray. The gas torch will be in such frequent use that it can stand out by the annealing pan; the flexible shaft machine, if you have one, is best mounted on the wall.

Some open shelving will be needed for jars of flux, enamel, buffing compounds, ammonia etc. Acid bottles should be racked to prevent them from falling off the shelf. A cupboard beneath the worktop is also useful for any bulkier equipment like an enamelling kiln or electric hotplate.

Transparent containers aid the identification of small pieces of different metals. Stacking plastic boxes are one solution; a do-it-yourself alternative is to hang old twist-cap jam jars beneath the lowest shelf (by screwing the caps securely on to the underside). Every scrap of metal should be jealously hoarded.

Lighting

Daylight is best, and plenty of it around the worktop. A long, thin horizontal window immediately above the worktop is good, or rooflights above it. Otherwise go for side light, watching out for equipment that might cause shadows. Good general artificial light is required, with local lighting for the central working area, the annealing tray and the buffing wheel. You might sometimes want to vary the intensity of the light over the working area at night, so an adjustable table lamp or perhaps a rise-and-fall fitting might be better than a spot. But a table lamp should be clamped to the edge, or bracketed on

the back wall, rather than standing on the table.

Jewellery is quite inactive and warm hands are vital for maximum sensitivity, so the room should be heated to between 18° and 30°C. It must be kept permanently dry to avoid rusting of tools; central heating or night storage, probably supplemented in some way while you are at work, will be excellent. Go for a heater with thermostatic controls to avoid having to make adjustments in the middle of tricky work.

Walls and floors

If you do not have pegboard behind the working areas, the local finish should be something you can occasionally wipe down, like ceramic or vinyl tiles or their equivalent. But this is not a vital requirement – jewellery does not normally throw up dirt or splashes. As to floors, absolutely anything will do. The only real reason for avoiding carpet might be inequality of wear. If dropped, metals show up more easily on dark colours.

Safety

The main safety risk in jewellery is acid. This must be handled properly – always added slowly to water, *never* the other way round. A vessel made of copper, nickel, brass or flame-proof glass should be used for the pickling solution, heated (if need be) on an electric rather than a gas ring. You should use the lid of the vessel to shield yourself against acid splash when you place a piece of work in the solution (using copper, nickel or brass tongs), and the lid – incorporating no corroding material – should at all times remain on the vessel to prevent inhalation of the fumes. Good ventilation is required. Non-corrosive pickling substances are available, and are perhaps more suitable for home use.

If you do splash acid, don't panic. If it is on your skin, head swiftly for the sink and flush it off, then neutralise with bicarbonate of soda (which should be kept

handy anyway for use after the pickling). If it is on your clothes, the worktop or the floor, apply bicarbonate of soda right away.

Be careful not to wear loose clothing when you are using the buffing wheel, especially near your neck, as you will be stooping over the wheel quite a bit. Long hair should be securely fastened up for the same reason. There should be an easily reached stop mechanism for the wheel in case of emergencies.

Other possible areas of risk are electric grinding (wear shatterproof goggles) and soldering (light the torch pointing away from you and remember the tip stays hot after the flame is put out). Treat all sharp tools with respect.

Keep a first-aid box within reach and have a fire extinguisher in the room.

Workshops

Even if power tools are not used, workshops tend to generate noise and dust, so they should be located outside the house wherever possible. A lean-to at the back of the house will not need planning permission, and can be bought in kit form for do-it-yourself building. The same goes for garden sheds, or you could convert an existing one, but in both cases remember the need for thermal insulation. If you have space at the end of your garage, see the section on dual-purpose rooms in Part One.

If you live in a listed building or for some other reason cannot contemplate an outside workshop, choose a room as far as possible from living areas, and preferably not with a party wall. Read the section on noise in Part One and decide how much you will have to do to make the place bearable. Make sure doors that connect with the rest of the house are sealed against escaping dust. Upstairs rooms are usually not ideal, because you will periodically have to cart heavy and messy materials through the house.

If you envisage installing ambitious machinery such as a circular saw, you will need a solid floor and noise insulation will become essential. A cellar might satisfy both these requirements, but nowhere else inside the house should be considered unless you are prepared to go in for some really rugged, structural noise-proofing.

Layout

Simple home workshops – excluding the sort of heavy machinery just mentioned – lend themselves to long narrow spaces where the worktop is confined to one wall, and the other used for storing sheet materials. Be sure this leaves you with enough standing room, though – capable of accommodating the width of a saw-horse and to spare. Doors at both ends are useful for manoeuvring long lengths of material on and off worktops and storage.

If two or more people are likely to use the workshop together, the choice will probably be between a double-sided peninsula bench or a back-to-back configuration. The first of these may prove better, as it leaves the walls free for storage, but either way a lot more space will be needed.

Furniture

Many home workshops just need one worktop, but it should be treated as an important piece of equipment. The height should be determined by the sort of work you are most likely to be doing. For most screwing, nailing, planing and some sawing, sanding and drilling, the 'general worktop' height applies – about 100mm below elbow height. But if the kind of work you will be doing involves a lot of downward pressure, or if you will often be working on large pieces, 200mm below elbow height is better.

There may be a case for having a split-level working surface, especially if you want to install machines such as a lathe or a multi-purpose woodworking machine. The working height of the machine (or, if several, the highest) should then be at elbow height, and the bench surface correspondingly lower. In practice this will probably mean two separate benches.

Benches need to be really solid and well braced, as long as space will allow and not less than 400mm wide. The legs should be at least 75 × 75mm, or the whole structure anchored to the wall. The top could be made of two layers of 19mm blockboard as an alternative to the solid pine or beech normally used. Several manufacturers make purpose-built work-benches, some including drawers, some fitted with tool slots at the rear. If you want to make your own, study the construction of these before you begin, and base your own design on them. If you buy a bench with a fitted vice, bear in mind that a top-mounted vice raises the actual working surface when the vice is in

use quite considerably, whereas a front-mounted vice keeps the work flush with the bench.

A stool may come in useful if you want to drop your eye level close to the bench for intermittent detailed work. You could run one up to suit your own height quickly and cheaply.

MIKE BENSON/MARSHALL CAVENDISH

Right: this large garden shed has plenty of room for use as a workshop, with strong adjustable shelving, a good-sized work-bench and a powered woodworking machine. Wall and roof insulation would make it more useful in winter.
Above: the workbench in the picture opposite is a simple but solid design intended for home construction.

Storage

This is probably the most important factor in designing your workshop, since clutter can be very limiting where large amounts of equipment and materials are shoe-horned into a small space.

Almost invariably the wall above the worktop is used for storing tools, generally on pegboard. Alternatively, screwdrivers, chisels and similar tools can be hung in grooves cut into wooden battens mounted on the wall. Small tools like drill bits generally stand in holes drilled into a wooden block. This can either stand free on the worktop, or a shelf above, or be provided as a lip at the back of the bench (slots in this lip can also act as sheaths for saws and other sharp tools). Where pegboard is used, it is a good idea to draw the outline of each tool on the board. Then you can see at a glance what is missing.

Shelving above the storage area should provide space for commonly used equipment – screws, nails, pots of glue, varnish, polish and so on. Modular nests of transparent plastic drawers are a good proprietary storage system for small objects, but it would be easier on the pocket to use jam jars, or twist-cap jars with the caps screwed to the underside of the lowest shelf. Shallow drawers may be useful for plans, templates etc.

Sheet materials should be stored upright against a wall or, less handily, in the rafters. If they are stored upright, a wooden batten should be securely fixed to the floor to prevent them slipping. Long pieces of timber, or metal rods, strips and angles should be stored flat, preferably on solid brackets fairly high up on the wall, or again in the rafters. Shorter pieces can be stored upright in a rack.

The space beneath the workbench is sometimes used for material storage, but it is best kept for bulky and less frequently used things like saw-horses. A good, big waste bin is vital and should be given uncovered space at one end of the bench. If it is roughly the width of the bench, rectangular and placed so that its rim is at bench height or just below, it will be possible to sweep waste into it with a minimum of spillage.

Lighting

You need good light in a workshop, but its source is not so important. Use fluorescent tubes to provide general lighting at night or if daylight is inadequate, and spots or suspended tungsten bulbs (with a shade that protects your eyes from the bulb) over working surfaces and all machines. If you can use daylight, a rooflight running the length of the bench (perhaps by using transparent plastic corrugated sheet) is ideal. If you have outside doors at both ends, fit ones with glazed panels, the upper panel louvred for extra ventilation as well as light.

Heating

Background heating coupled with thermal insulation is important, as much for the tools as for you. They will rust if the workshop isn't kept dry. The room temperature when you are working need not be high, as a lot of physical activity will be involved, but the sort of flexibility provided by a wall-mounted fan heater will cater for sedentary periods. Remember that warm hands are safer, as well as more comfortable, than cold ones.

Walls and floors

Hard floor coverings should be chosen for any workshop; in a woodwork shop sweeping up will be the main form of cleaning, so any finish will do. In a metal-work shop oil may be spilled, so porous surfaces should be avoided, and so should natural rubber (but synthetic rubber is not vulnerable to oil). Vinyl sheet or tiles are a good surface, especially if coved at the edges to run 200–300mm up the walls. In a plastics workshop, resin and other chemicals may get spilt, so check the vulnerability of different floor coverings to specific materials you may be using. Asphalt is probably the safest bet for all-round resistance. See also the notes on welding below. Walls may not show much behind all the storage, but a light-coloured gloss paint is recommended.

*Benches and shelving of any shape can be
made up from metal angle. Here, general
tools are kept safe and tidy on simple racks
made from wood battens and nails, screwed
to the wall above the bench.*

Waste disposal

Wood can be burnt, but if you live in a smokeless zone, you may have to arrange for special waste collections. Local authorities dislike swarf and metal filings showing up in household refuse, so the same applies here. Plastic waste can be burnt if there is no toxicity risk, but can produce an awful smell, so you may have to make arrangements for periodic collection by a specialist disposal firm. Some plastics (acrylic for example) have some scrap value if you can find a specialised dealer, who may also turn out to be a source of raw materials.

Safety

To avoid clutter, as much as for safety, tools should be returned to their storage immediately after use, even if they are going to be used again shortly – especially sharp tools that might get hidden under waste or accidentally knocked off the bench.

Electrical equipment should be connected to nearby power points so as to keep vulnerable lengths of flex as short as possible. A continuous power track on the ceiling or beneath the lowest shelf has advantages in this context.

Good outside ventilation is essential in plastics workshops where toxic chemicals may be used, and protective clothing may also be called for (for example gloves if using peroxide, the catalyst for GRP).

Fires with open flames should not be used in wood or plastics workshops. A dry powder fire extinguisher should be kept within easy reach of the bench in all workshops. See also under welding below. A first-aid box, prominently identified, should be kept within easy reach of the workbench.

Welding

This is potentially the most dangerous operation encountered in a leisure room, and special precautions are needed against fire, and to protect the user. What follows is a guide, but local fire regulations should be carefully checked – they may be more stringent.

Welding should be done in fireproof surroundings, with all inflammable materials removed from within 10 metres. If this is impossible, as it is likely to be in most workshops and metal sculptors' studios, the welding areas should be screened off with asbestos or metal sheeting. Don't forget the floor and the ceiling. Concrete, quarry, brick and similar floors are safe, but timber and finished surfaces are not. If they cannot be avoided, they should be shielded likewise. Ceilings must be shielded if there is any doubt as to their fire-resistance. Polystyrene tiles are especially dangerous in this context.

The welding table should be of metal frame construction, with a metal or fire-brick surface. In oxy-acetylene welding,

the cylinders must either stand in a stout rack anchored to a wall, or be secured to the wall by a chain. When moving cylinders, handle them carefully and do not roll them. Do not stand in front of the cylinder valves when you are opening them, and do not open the acetylene valve more than one turn. Leave the wrench in the acetylene valve for an emergency shutdown (acetylene is always shut off first).

Protective clothing for oxy-acetylene welding comprises leather gloves and a pair of welding goggles, but it is wise to avoid loose clothing and to wear a pair of boots as well. Electric-arc welding throws off harmful rays, and protective clothing should include leggings and sleeves of asbestos cloth, a leather apron, gauntlet gloves and a wrap-round face mask. Do-it-yourself welding kits usually include basic protective gear, but make sure goggles are fitted with the correct lenses.

A damp floor should be avoided when electric-arc welding, and good ventilation is important. The voltage output is relatively low, so the risk of serious electric shock is small, but you should not tinker with the equipment if it breaks down, and especially not with the transformer.

You should never flame-cut into metal containers if they held inflammable materials or if you do not know what they held, as the residue could cause an explosion. Never use oil or grease on welding equipment.

You must have an adequate fire extinguisher handy, and it would be wise to supplement this with buckets of sand. Do not use a water-based extinguisher or water itself to put out a fire in an area where there is electrical equipment.

 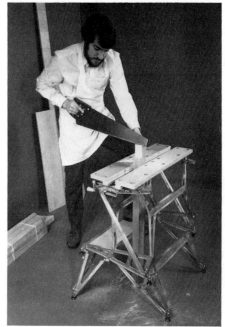

The Black & Decker Workmate consists of a large vice mounted on a stable frame. It will handle almost any object, is adjustable in height, and folds up out of the way when not in use.

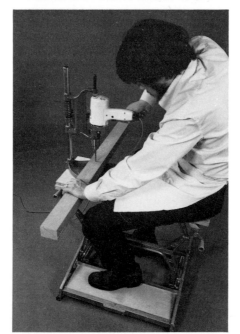 

Model-making

Model-making here refers to boat, aircraft and architectural modelling, characteristically in light wood like balsa. There are other kinds of modelling, of course, but these have more in common with other kinds of leisure room – metal modelling has much the same requirements as a fully fledged metal workshop, and clay modelling needs a room like a potter's studio.

Your choice of room depends first on whether you will be test-running small engines. If so, you will need good outside ventilation and you will be making a lot of noise. So choose a room that does not have a party wall if possible, and do some basic noise insulation on all the walls (see noise section in Part One).

Even so, and not forgetting to seal the door against fumes as well as noise, you may trouble neighbours with the sound that escapes through the open windows or ventilators (though soundproof ventilators are available). You can muffle this crudely by building test boxes out of a reasonably dense material and lining them with fibreglass blanket, retained by chicken-wire. This will also mop up some effluent. The engines themselves should be fitted with silencers.

All the above applies just as much to an out-house. If you have the chance to build one for the purpose, try and present blank walls to the directions in which noise would do most harm.

Layout

Storing finished and half-finished models is likely to be a more critical use of space than building them, and this should be a factor in your choice of room as well as its layout. If the ceiling is high enough, suspending them is a practical possibility. Otherwise you may need deep, bulky rack or cupboard shelving. If the room is large enough, concentrate building operations at one end, and use the spare floor area for storage.

It follows from all this that a loft would make a good model-maker's room, since it would probably combine a certain amount of roof storage along the ridge with up to 40 per cent of otherwise redundant floor space.

Furniture

Two worktops are needed – a standing bench for building the models, and either a desk and chair or a free-standing drawing board for designing. The bench should be at 'general worktop' height (100mm below elbow height) since high structures are not involved and downward pressure rarely required. Solid construction is needed for the bench, but not to the extent of a woodwork shop; a sturdy, old kitchen table would probably be adequate.

Proprietary drawing desks can be bought in which the drawing board folds down flush with the adjoining surface to increase worktop space, which might be useful; alternatively you can probably devise something yourself which will do the job just as well on an ordinary table. Since most of the work done at this desk will be drawing, you should let the height of the drawing board dictate the height of the desk. This depends somewhat on the board's slope, and is ultimately a matter of personal comfort, but as a first suggestion, try 100–150mm below elbow height.

Storage

Apart from storing finished and partly assembled models as described under 'Layout', you will need shelving for tools, glue, paint and reference books. Pegboard is a possible way of storing tools but a shallow slotted shelf may be more suitable, as model-makers' tools are mostly small. A drilled wood block is useful for drill bits. Shallow drawers can be mounted beneath the worktop to hold plans, sheet material and any equipment not kept on the shelves.

Lighting

Daylight is preferable, as much of the work is fiddly and detailed. For night work, a mix of good general light and local spots is suitable. If an adjustable table lamp is preferred on account of its greater flexibility, it should be clamped to the table or mounted on a wall-bracket, not left standing where it could get knocked over. A continuous power track is a good idea, and if the roof is too high for convenience, it can be run under the lowest shelf above the worktop.

Heating

Model-making is not very strenuous, so a fairly high temperature (18–20°C) is needed to keep the hands warm. There are no constraints on how this is achieved except that naked flames are best avoided because of the risk of inflammable dust and paint vapour.

RICHARD DRAPER

Walls and floors

Almost any floor finish is suitable except carpet, which is vulnerable to balsa cement and difficult to clear of minute shavings. It is possible to carpet most of the room, with just a strip of hard floor-covering in front of the worktop, though. Choose light colours for the walls if you need to reflect daylight around the room. The choice of wall finish is not critical, though the area above the worktop may need the protection of something like ceramic tiles, vinyl, sealed cork or plastic laminate.

Safety

Model-making is pretty safe, but care should be taken with sharp tools. Replace them in their storage immediately after use. Minimise flex lengths on electrical appliances and provide a vertical rack for the soldering iron so it can't inadvertently burn you or your materials. Keep a small first-aid kit handy for minor cuts, and a fire extinguisher as model engine fuels and paints are highly inflammable.

A converted loft makes a good room for a model-maker, with plenty of storage space for completed models under the ridge of the roof and cupboards in the spaces left under its slope.

Printing and dyeing

This section is primarily about fabric printing and dyeing; although some of the techniques are shared with printing on paper (and to that extent it will be relevant to these activities), it is reasonable to assume that lithography and full-scale printing presses are beyond most people's hobby budgets.

Size and water supply are the two main criteria in choosing a room for printing or dyeing. Size is all-important for printing and it is possible, although inconvenient, to bring in water as needed if your pocket won't stretch to additional plumbing. For dyeing, room size is relatively unimportant but availability of water much more so, as large volumes are involved. If you have any choice left after considering these factors, go for the room with the best daylight.

Layout
The reason why the size of room is important in printing is that you will need a table slightly larger than the largest print you will want to make, and because you will need to work on both sides of it, except for the smallest prints. In many cases the room (and therefore the printing table it will accommodate) will effectively determine the maximum size of your prints for you, and if you have no space for a peninsula printing table, you will be severely limited. Ideally the table should be located so that you have access all round it, but if necessary one end can be pushed up against a wall.

The progression in printing is: drawing; preparation of blocks, screens, inks etc; printing; drying; storage of finished prints. Drying and storage of prints should be carefully segregated from the preparation area, preferably by housing them on opposite sides of the printing table, so that you have distinct 'clean' and 'dirty' zones fitting into the sequence of operations. Where you then place the drawing board depends on space. Drawings

should be kept clean too, but since they are logically related to the preparation area, it makes sense to keep them fairly close – perhaps at one end of a fairly long worktop.

Dyeing is less demanding altogether. For tie-dyeing, you need only a small clean area for preparing the material, a sink, the dyebath and space for drying. An ironing board in the room would be useful, too, but not essential. It is logical to follow the sequence just described in laying out the room, but remember that you have to double back to the sink to rinse the material after dyeing, so keep it a reasonable distance from the preparation area where undyed material might get splashed or dripped on.

Batik follows broadly the same sequence, except that you need a larger worktop incorporating a separate gas or electric ring to keep the wax molten, and either this or a separate worktop must be large enough to accommodate the full width of the material when you are ironing off the wax between layers of newspaper. A separate table for this purpose is definitely preferable.

Furniture
The printing table for both block and screen printing needs to be really solid and of a considerable size – not the sort of furniture, unfortunately, that you can usually pick up second-hand. You may already know the maximum size of the work you will want to do, or this may become clear from the only room you have available. But as a rough guide, the table should be 150mm larger all round than the largest print, and for printed textiles should not be much less than 1800 × 1200mm. You will need to apply downward pressure, so it should stand 200mm beneath the elbows. It should be covered with an old blanket, then a couple of layers of newspaper, and then a resilient material like oilcloth, stretched taut and secured round the edges. For screen printing, the rubberised blanket available

for the purpose from specialist suppliers is best.

Other worktops in a printing room should be as long as the space allows, up to 900mm wide for screen printing, where you will be handling screens not much smaller than the printing table itself, but only about 400mm for block printing, and standing at or just below elbow height. You may wish to build in a fold-down drawing board at the appropriate end of the worktop.

The worktop needed for dyeing should be about the same height and width as that for block printing, and a minimum of 600mm long for tie-dyeing and double that for batik. If a free-standing clothes boiler is being used for the dyeing, its rim should be 25mm below the elbow – as should the sink. If a table-mounted boiler is used, remember that you will need a bucket beneath its outlet (using a hose to prevent splashing). The ironing table for batik should be 100–200mm below below elbow height to give reasonable pressure.

In the preparation stages of both printing and batik, there may be times when you would like the work to be closer to your eyes for fine detail. The size of the work makes a portion of raised worktop impractical, so you may need a stool which will lower your eyes, when seated, to within 300mm of the surface.

Storage

In printing, you will need fairly bulky storage in the 'clean' zone for drying and storing prints. The best device is a specialised rack system in which prints are held vertically, tautened between ball bearings at top and bottom. This is available from specialist suppliers. A low-budget alternative is to use bulldog clips suspended from a line or fixed rail, but this is strictly second best. If you don't buy or devise some sort of vertical drying area, you will quickly find prints littering every available horizontal surface, to your subsequent frustration.

For printed textiles, batiks and tie-dyed materials, an old-fashioned kitchen pulley is ideal, provided that you have enough ceiling space and that the area beneath is not vulnerable to a few drips. Failing this, a free-standing, expanding clothes-horse will do, or the sort of pull-out drying line that is popular in small bathrooms.

Permanent storage of paper prints, if not displayed on the wall, is best provided by wide, shallow drawers. A chest of these can also be used to keep drawing paper. Printed textiles, batiks and tie-dyed materials can be folded or kept in drawers, rolled and stood in vertical racks, or kept inside cardboard or plastic tubes (these would not harm paper prints, either, if they cannot be stored flat) which in turn can be kept upright or horizonally on racks.

Tools, dyes, paints, inks, wax and similar 'dirty' substances should be stored close to the worktops with which they are associated. A length of pegboard on the wall behind the worktop is appropriate for larger tools (for block printing, or if you make your own screens and squeegees). Brushes, bottles, tins and so forth should be stored either in drawers beneath the worktop or on open shelves.

In dyeing, storage for dyes and solvents should be provided close to the sink or the dyebath and not allowed to stray over into the preparation area, where the only storage needed is for string and rubber bands (for tie-dyeing), or janting needles and brushes (for batik). Janting needles should have their own box in which they are wedged separately with foam in a straightforward progression of sizes. Brushes should be kept flat in trays, if in drawers, or heads upward in jars, if on shelves.

Photographic screens

If you aim to use photographic screens in screen-printing, you will need to be able to black out all natural light, as in a photographic darkroom. See the section on darkrooms for how to do this. You will also need gas or electric rings for heating distilled water and glycerine.

Lighting
Try to plan the room so that the maximum daylight falls on the preparation areas in both printing and dyeing and then (in printing) on the printing table. In dyeing, the worktop can face the window, but if it is much more than a strip, it will restrict wall storage, so side light will probably turn out to be better. In printing you should take care that maximising daylight at the preparation area will not inadvertently mean that you sometimes work in your own shadow at the printing table. Rooflights are, of course, ideal.

Artificial lighting should be a mixture of good general light, and local light at dyebaths, worktops, drawing boards and the sink. Spots are suitable for all but the printing table, where the light should be evenly distributed over the whole surface, rather like a billiard table. A well shaded fluorescent tube hung quite low over the centre of the table is excellent, but experiment with the height until you cut out reflected glare.

Heating
Neither printing nor dyeing is particularly physical, though printing may be more active if you make your own screens and squeegees. Also the environment can be affected quite significantly by gas or electric rings. Thermostatically controlled heat should provide a minimum 18°C; the warmer the room, the faster prints and dyed cloths will dry. If metal tools are used, the room must be kept dry at all times.

Walls and floors
Light-coloured finishes will help to distribute daylight. An easily wiped-down finish like gloss paint is suitable for walls except round sinks, dyebaths and 'dirty zone' worktops, where something tougher like vinyl or ceramic tiles is better. Floors should be able to take a good scrub. Non-porous solid floors (which are more resistant to staining) or vinyl are both satisfactory.

Safety
Apart from routine precautions when using sharp tools (for making blocks), batik workers in particular should remember that molten wax is highly inflammable. See the note on safety in the section on candle-making. You should also be careful with glycerine, which is used in photographic screen-printing.

Candle-making

If candle-making is just a temporary fad of your children, you will probably have to grin and bear it in the kitchen, as it does require access to a gas or electric ring (preferably several) and a sink, and it would scarcely be worth providing these specially. But if you are thinking of taking up candle-making more seriously – perhaps to sell to local craft shops, and to stockpile for Christmas – you may find yourself spending long hours at it, in which case the kitchen is really not the right place.

Candle-making does not, in fact, take up a lot of room. It can be doubled up with a spare bedroom or any kind of room in which there is space for a reasonable worktop. Although some people cool candles in water baths, it is not essential or even desirable to do this (embedding the mould in sand produces better results), so a sink is not strictly necessary. But it is very useful to have water for cleaning messy moulds, and a room with a sink would be an advantage.

Layout

This is simple – the progression is from the hotplate, where the wax is melted, across a worktop where the candle is formed, to the sand-bed (or possibly water bath) in which the candle is cooled. The working area – which can be along one wall – should be laid out to reflect this sequence.

Furniture

You may conceivably have an old cooker lying around which could be pressed into service as a heat source, but most people will start off with one or two electric or gas rings which can be bought up second-hand provided you have an expert check them over before they're fitted. The more rings you have, the more colours you can have on the go at once, and therefore the more versatile you are. See under safety overleaf.

The worktop should be at least 1200mm long if it is carrying burners at one end, or half this if a free-standing cooker is being used. A width of 400mm will probably be quite adequate, and the surface should be about 100mm beneath the elbows. A second-hand kitchen table, perhaps adjusted for height, will do. It will get stained abominably, so if there is a reason to disguise its function, cover it with newspaper when you work. For fine decoration you might find it useful to have a stool which will temporarily lower your eyes nearer to the worktop.

Storage
You need to store wax, moulds, some basic tools (scissors, craft knife, butane torch, and perhaps even a power tool), dyes, lengths of wick, sand and, of course, finished candles. A mixture of open shelves and dust-proof cupboards is likely to be the best answer, though there may be something to be said for keeping your tools on pegboard above the worktop. Anything that should be kept clean, such as wax, moulds, sand and wicks, should be kept in the cupboards, but open shelves are the ideal place for finished candles, and decorative to boot. Wrap them in transparent plastics 'cling film' to keep them spotless if they are going to be sold or used as Christmas presents. If you are dipping candles or tapers, you will need a judiciously placed line or rod where they can be hung to set.

Lighting
Daylight is an advantage, especially when working with different colours, but not essential. The room should otherwise have good background lighting supplemented by local light at the working area. Since this space is quite compact and homogeneous, a fluorescent tube suspended above the length of the worktop, or mounted beneath the lowest shelf above it, might turn out to be an efficient solution. It should be operated by a pull-cord rather than a switch.

Heating
Candle-making is not a particularly vigorous activity, so the room should be well heated while you are working, though background heat need only be enough to stop tools rusting. The gas or electric rings will affect the room temperature, so a quick-response, thermostatically controlled heater is required.

Walls and floors
The wall area immediately above the worktop should be finished in a tough, easily cleaned material with resistance to dye-stains, such as ceramic tiles or vinyl. A scrubbable hard floor-covering should be used for the area immediately in front of the worktop (vinyl is again a good choice) but this need not be extended to the rest of the room if, for instance, it is also used as a bedroom.

Safety
Wax seems so workaday, it can be deceptive. In fact it is a serious fire risk, and precautions should be taken accordingly. Wax that drips around the gas or electric rings should be chipped off every day when cold; alternatively, shape aluminium foil round the burners each day and simply throw it away when you have finished. Always heat wax in a double-boiler, or equivalent, and use asbestos mats on the burners themselves in case of direct drips (very easy to do). Keep raw and waste wax well away from heat sources. Wear leather gloves when pouring wax at high temperatures, and keep a foam fire extinguisher close by.

Candles must not be knocked while they are cooling – for their sake as well as for yours. For this reason again, sand is a better cooling medium than water as the candles are more stable when they are embedded in it.

Home brewing

Successive Chancellors of the Exchequer have done wonders for this hobby, and it has now completely lost its hitherto somewhat rustic associations. This review assumes that you will be going through the whole process of home brewing or wine-making, but these days it is possible to buy ready-prepared kits which cut out one or two stages of this process, in which case your requirements will be correspondingly less.

Many home brewers use the kitchen for preparing their must or wort, and another room to keep steeping, fermenting, racked or bottled liquor. The advantage of the kitchen is that it already has some essential needs – gas or electric rings and a water supply. But it is better for both you and your brews if you can minimise the amount of lugging around you have to do,

The kitchen is usually where most home brewing is done, and if there is room for short-term storage of fermenting wines and beers this will simplify the process.

so it is more convenient if you can do everything in the one room. The larger this room is, the more ambitious you can be. Obviously at least a cold water supply is highly desirable.

Layout

The sequence of activities in both brewing and wine-making is broadly the same – from boiling, steeping or mashing, through fermentation, to racking and ultimately to bottling. The layout of the room should try to reflect this sequence. It might at first seem logical to divide the room between 'operations' and 'storage', but in fact the short-term storage needed for steeping and fermenting is associated more with the preparation of the liquor than with the long-term storage after racking and bottling. In any case, this long-term storage is generally better done in a colder, darker place than the brewing room itself. The ideal layout of the preparation area would therefore be: burners (or boiler), worktop, short-term storage, sink.

Furniture

A good solid worktop is an important requirement for home brewing, which often involves heavy vessels and some downward pressure. Its dimensions depend on the likely volume of your output, whether you are using free-standing burners (or a cooker) or boiler, and whether you use part of the worktop itself for storing vessels containing steep-ing or fermenting liquor.

If all these apply, do not think in terms of a worktop much smaller than 1800 × 500mm. Its height may depend on the size of the vessels you are using, but 200mm below elbow height is unlikely to be too low for mashing, stirring a heavy wort, manipulating fruit presses and moving heavy fruit pans on and off burners.

The worktop is likely to get stained, so there is little point spending a lot of money on it. An old kitchen table or any-thing similar from a junk shop should fit the bill, provided that it is sturdy enough. If you need two tables to make up sufficient working area, make sure they are the same height. Further up the price scale, modular kitchen units, bought in kit form, provide the right dimensions for a lot of people and incorporate useful cupboard space.

The sink may be a problem. If placed at its ideal height, it will be well above the worktop, which is unsightly, but more important will mean lifting heavy vessels over the rim. The sort of compromise found in fitted kitchens (where the sink is flush with the worktop) is perhaps justified here because you will often be working at the height of a bottle or gallon jar, plus funnel, above the sink bottom. It is important to get taps fitted well above the sink, or to have an outlet that can be swivelled aside, out of the way of large glass vessels.

Storage

There are two different requirements here – short-term storage during fermentation, and long-term storage after racking and bottling. Fermentation vessels tend to be heavy, and they need to come back to the preparation area when fermentation is finished. The best storage for them is therefore close to the worktop and at the same height. In fact, if worktop space permits they can simply be stood at one end of it, between the preparation area and the sink, where racking and bottling will take place. However the heat of the room during fermentation plays a critical role, and in some rooms a special fermentation cupboard will be needed (see below).

For long-term storage, the brewing room is not ideal at all, and should be avoided if possible. A constant tempera-ture of 10–13°C is recommended for maturing wine, and this would be too cold to work in. A cellar is, of course, the best thing of all; failing that, a garage with insulation to prevent the beer or wine from

Long-term storage can be cooler than normal room temperatures. Failing a cellar, an insulated garage or shed will do well if the temperature is even and never falls below 5°C.

dropping below 5°C, or the coolest dark corner within the house (under the stairs?). Darkness is especially important for red wine, and in a garage bottles should be wrapped in blankets or newspaper to keep the light out. If the brewing room has to be used, the bottles should be stored in light-proof cupboards, either filled up to the cork and standing upright, or on their sides in a simple rack to keep the corks moist.

Equipment should be stored in cupboards or on shelves above or beneath the worktop. Since it will all have to be sterilised before use, the marginally greater cleanliness of cupboards is not terribly important. Vessels that are too big for wall-mounted shelves can simply be kept on the floor beneath the worktop. Try to relate storage 'zones' to the preparation sequence described under layout.

Lighting

Good general lighting is important, though whether this is from outside or from an artificial source matters little. It may need to be supplemented at the worktop if you find yourself peering at hydrometers etc. In the 'cellar' a 40W, unshaded, clear glass bulb is best for checking on the clarity of maturing wine. Pull-cords rather than switches are recommended in the brewing room.

Heating

Home brewing is not totally sedentary, nor particularly active, so a working temperature of 16–18°C is indicated. The lower of these temperatures is also the minimum efficient temperature for wine fermentation, so room temperature should be maintained constantly by central heating, night storage, or an equivalent method if you are storing fermenting vessels in the open. If this is impossible, or too expensive, you will need an extra piece of furniture – an insulated cupboard in which a constant temperature can be maintained by a low wattage heater.

If you are not likely to be fermenting a lot at a time, you could replace this cupboard by using a tea-chest lined with an insulating blanket, and an electric light bulb will then probably provide enough heat. Beer ferments at lower temperatures – not more than 16°C for bitter and mild; 10°C during the first three days and 5°C thereafter for lager (this temperature may have to be maintained for up to six months!).

Walls and floors

Splashes are likely to occur in the area of the worktop and the sink, so ceramic or vinyl wall tiles or something similarly resistant to stains are a good idea. Otherwise the type of wall finish does not really matter, though a gloss paint will wipe down easily in case of explosions! The floor should have a hard finish that can be washed easily – non-porous solid floors are one possibility, but are more likely to shatter dropped glass vessels than something a trifle more resilient such as foam-backed vinyl or sealed cork tiles.